What People Are Saying about Michele Lando

"Michele is a partner that walks her talk and 'lives the brand.' Her knowledge, and her ability to navigate between leadership and support teams, combined with her deep understanding of our company and all the people in it, made her an invaluable team member / partner. I would gladly partner with Michele again and confidently recommend her brand strategy, marketing and sales/speaking services to anyone wanting a true partnership to move the dial for their company!"

Jason Burlie, VP Sales and Marketing
MullinTBG, A Prudential Financial company

"Having attended your IndiBrand™, Individual Branding, training program some years ago I knew of your capabilities which prompted me to phone you regarding my most current post-merger/acquisition cultural integration and teambuilding needs. I recognized that 1/3 of our department's team was 'new' in the last 12 months and that realizing our business goals would require that our team perform as a seasoned and integrated unit. We needed to short circuit the timeframe. You were our secret weapon.

"Your program exceeded our expectations. We have never had a more responsive and engaged offsite and, as you experienced, they couldn't get enough and literally extended your program on the spot by consensus!"

Dennis Moore, Chief Marketing Officer
Houlihan Lokey

"Michele is a very astute business person, yet one of the most charming and dynamic human beings I've ever met. She has tremendous strategic thinking ability, combined with the ability to know just how to execute business strategy in branding, marketing and general communications. She's also a fearless, tireless and ethical business leader, able to weather many market and financial ups and downs.

"I would hire Michele, work for Michele, work with Michele and generally accept her thoughtful and caring business guidance on pretty much any occasion again."

Beth Vanni, Channel Vice President
Cisco Systems, Inc.

"I was one of the students listening to your talk when you visited Paula Woodley's class a couple weeks ago. I really loved it when you spoke about introspection; I even wrote down your point that 'we're unaware of our innate uniqueness and undervalue it because it's already a part of us.' I scribbled it in my notebook because I never thought of my self worth that way! I even told one of my best friends here what you had said and she had to pause because it blew her away as well. That line has been stuck in my head ever since, so I thank you for your advice. I feel that it will stick with me for a long time."

Monique Manaloto, student
University of Southern California

"Michele Lando is a true partner. When working with her Brand, Marketing and Sales Training Agency, Skilset Communications, you forget she is not part of your internal team. She is strategic with big picture vision and brand leadership ability that transfers through to marketing and sales in-the-field tactics. Moreover, she is completely committed to looking out for your / your firms' best interests at all times.

"I 'inherited' her firm's partnership when I was brought in to run Sales and Marketing for MullinTBG, then a newly-acquired firm within Prudential Retirement. She met all of our goals and beyond. Given such a positive and successful experience working with her, I brought her on board to assist with positioning, messaging, sales tool development and go-to-market strategy in my current role as EVP of the CitizensTrust Division of Citizens Business Bank."

Dan Banis, EVP and Head of CitizensTrust

"Michele Lando has the uncanny ability to quickly discover the heart of your message and craft it in ways you can't imagine. She's insightful, wildly creative, and no nonsense. The value she added to our marketing efforts far exceeded our expectations."

Eyvette A. Jones, Founder and Executive Director
Urban Possibilities

"Michele Lando's presentation at a recent Pacific Life confer-
ence was the finest presentation of any kind I have seen in a
long time. She is engaging, easily connects with her audience
and communicates her topic clearly and effectively. For the first
time I have a clear understanding of the value and importance
of branding. When she finished I wanted more of what she has
to offer and am doing additional work with her. If you are going to hear her speak you are in for a treat."

Jeffrey Hales, Managing Partner
Hawthorne Financial, L.L.C.

"Attending Michele's training was invaluable. My objective is
to add 'value' to client visits. Identifying my personal value was
eye-opening and made me realize that my personal brand in
fact differentiated me from my competitors, resulting in in-
creased confidence."

Pam Hauk, CLU, ChFC, formerly Field Vice President,
M Marketing, Pacific Life

CREATE DEMAND FOR YOUR BRAND...

FROM THE INSIDE OUT

CREATE DEMAND FOR YOUR BRAND...

FROM THE INSIDE OUT

HOW TO ALIGN YOUR PURPOSE, PASSION AND PROFIT

Michele Lando

Amazon #1 Bestselling Author

Create Demand for Your Brand... From the Inside Out: How to Align Your Purpose, Passion and Profit

© 2017 Michele Lando

Skilset Communications, Inc.
556 S. Fair Oaks Avenue, Suite 101
Pasadena, CA 91105

ISBN: 978-0-9991543-0-4

This book is only possible because of my mentor, my biggest fan and active supporter — a truly extraordinary human being we are all blessed to have in our lives and that I get to call my husband, Manny (Manuel João Paiva).

My mother, who is within me every day and who stood in front, behind and beside me with wisdom, laughter and a full heart for her family.

And to Jax, a reminder that everything is possible... and there's no reason to wait!

Contents

Part One - Discovery

The Journey Within   3

The Power of Purpose   13

Part Two - Your Roadmap

Step One: Introspection — from the Inside Out   21

Step Two: Differentiation — Why You?   37

Step Three: Your Unique Message   51

Step Four: Creating Brand Buzz — Let Your Purpose Guide You 73

Step Five: Maintenance — Aligning Your CHOICEs   101

About Michele Lando   131

Hire Michele To Speak At Your Event!   133

About Skilset Programs and Workshops   135

References   139

Acknowledgments

I have deep gratitude for so many people who have contributed to me and thereby to this book. A few simply cannot go without mention, because if not for them I wouldn't have the life stories, work experience and wisdom I have to offer.

To my mentors: I am forever grateful for Manny Paiva, Beverly Lando, Dr. Tessa Warschaw and Karen Harvey. I would have considered myself fortunate to have any one of you in my life. To have had four mentors I recognize has been beyond good fortune and is truly a blessing.

To my lifelong advocates and personal board of directors: Dianne Gubin, Deborah Seller, Akemi Harrington-Lai, Monica Santino, Char Meyer, Ben Adelman and Nikki Robischon, who have been with me through it all, held me accountable and always saw the best in me, even when not wearing rose-colored glasses.

My invaluable support system over the past two decades: Michelle "Shelly" Schaup, Mishele "Mimi" Vieira, Kelly Bunkley; as well as newcomers Eric and Skip and my editor,

Victoria St. George of Just Write Editorial & Literary Services, LLC.

To my husband's family, who have long ago become my own, most especially Paolo Paiva: you all live in my heart, my soul and my pen.

To a few noteworthy clients who allowed me to be my best and do my best work with them: Bill Page, Beth Vanni, Akemi Harrington, Nancy Duenkel, John Warren, Carmie Saldana, Jay Welker, JoAnn Anderson, Fung Der, Mike Shute, Kristi Barens, Dan Banis, Jason Burlie, Yong Lee, Eric Lucero, Dianne Snedaker, Mollie Richardson, Jennifer Leung, Kelly Johnston, Bobbi Becker, Hiroko Tatebe and the countless others who have invited me in, I thank you all! You have enriched my life.

I think it's equally important to acknowledge a few who influenced my journey's course directly with their teachings: Paul Larson, Eric LaBrecque, Tony Robbins and Bill Bonstetter, along with many others whom I have never met but have studied and learned much from just the same.

And finally in memory of my loving, playful and infectiously laughing father, David Lando and my sister, Cindy Lando, who left us far too soon. You both have gifted me with the knowledge there is so much more to life than what exists on this plane.

To the countless others who have contributed to my life's journey and fulfillment of living in my purpose: you are just too numerous to note but you know who you are and how very grateful I am!

PART ONE

Discovery

The Journey Within

> *"Knowing yourself is the beginning of all wisdom."*
>
> — ARISTOTLE

OVER THE PAST 20 YEARS I have had the great pleasure of working with and alongside tens of thousands of people who have wanted to achieve greater success. And we've been able to achieve this together. Moreover, and most inspirationally to the writing of this book, many of these people have confided in me their longing to know their purpose. In truth, sometimes *because* they had achieved phenomenal success, they realized there had to be more. Their financial success revealed the gap that still existed within.

Said another way, their notion that money was the end game and would be what brought them satisfaction was not accurate. I've heard this awakening expressed in many ways: "I thought if only I (made enough money, achieved certain status, became a leader in my company or my community, was an excellent parent, etc.), I would feel fulfilled."

I've built my life and my career fully embracing the concept that the best scenario, and in fact, the *only* path acceptable based on decades of experience, is when we align that yearning to know our life's purpose with how we go about living our daily lives. And that certainly includes integrating purpose into our work-life as well.

Purpose + Passion + Profit =
Fulfilling our Potential and Living Life Fully

There are moments in each of our lives that touch and define us. They come sometimes quietly, seemingly innocently, and sometimes they show up loudly, overtly and undeniably. I call these "markers": critical moments in our lives that act as clues to illuminate our purpose deep within. They aid us in our journey to self-discovery. If you don't know what your markers are, not to worry — we will explore them together throughout the book.

Some of my markers involve:

- the first "coaching" request I received at eight years of age
- achieving extraordinary and utterly unforeseeable sales success
- the courage to examine myself deeply and come out the other side time and again
- the most recent loss in my life, my mother, which leads me to why I am writing this book....

My Mother's Legacy

The importance of understanding my own purpose was always present at some level, and it grew as I began navigating my career and realizing where my satisfaction was best met. It continued to grow when coaching my clients and hearing what was missing for them. But it was undeniable that I was on a mission to help others understand their Purpose in 2010. That was the year my mother died.

When my mother was living with my husband and myself, my husband (who had already retired) really stepped up to be the caregiver so that I could continue with my career. I felt extremely lucky to have married a whole human being, great guy and a true partner. My husband would take my mother to most of her doctor's appointments. But on some occasions we knew that there were certain appointments where I just needed to go, and this was one of those appointments.

In the doctor's office that day, mom's doctor was, let's say, in a position that would be north on the compass. My mother was south, my husband was west and I was east. The doctor looked at my mother and said, "We have found that you have a problem with your heart valve. If you were in good health — for example, if you weren't on oxygen and you didn't have lung issues — we would operate and you would recover and move forward. But, in your case, because your lungs are so weak, it isn't possible for us to operate on you. You won't survive the operation.

"And so, what that means is, you have perhaps six months to live."

My mother was facing the doctor, and she gave a very slight tip of the head, not even a full nod, but as if to say, "I've heard you, and I understand."

Familiar to all of us are those times in life when you're in a conversation with someone, in any setting, and there's a silent pause and you feel the need to fill the silence. It's just an awkward moment.

Well, I can only imagine how awkward that moment was for the doctor. The courage it takes to have to tell someone, "You're going to die in x amount of time," is enormous. And when someone is silent, it must be very awkward to not fill the space. So the doctor, a woman about 39 years of age, leaned in to my mother and said, "Are you afraid?"

And my mother's response was: "No. I'm not afraid. I'm worried about my daughter. She's lost her father, her sister and now me. She won't have any family."

I was seated to the right of my mom and my mouth just fell open, and then I said, "Mom, I'm not going to like it, but I'm going to get through it. The last thing that you need to do right now is be worrying about me. Even in this moment, you are 'such a mom.' "

I think the doctor was just dumbfounded at my mother's selflessness. She went quiet, and we then turned and walked out of her office.

A couple of days went by, and we were sitting at the sun room in my house having a morning cup of coffee when my mother looked at me and said, "I guess I didn't make too much of my life." I realized that she had been ruminating for two-and-a-half days in silence — self-examining, self-questioning, going through whatever process she was going through, suffering silently. I was equal parts stunned by her and devastated for her.

My knee-jerk reaction was, "Mom, you and I just don't see this the same way. For me, I see you as a rock star. You told me all your life that all you ever wanted was a family, to raise a family. You came from a situation where at age 10 you were babysitting your little two-year-old nephew and he got ill and died a week later. Your brother was killed in a car accident when you were 11 years old. Your mother died when you were 14. Your father sold your home when you were 17 and you were on your own after that.

"Your entire life was built around creating the family that you didn't have, creating the childhood for your children that you never experienced. It was your passion. It was your purpose. And you did it beyond my wildest expectations. And I certainly would be the one to take the measure because I was the recipient of it."

With tears now fully flowing and my speech getting faster, I added: "You were so attentive. You were so available. You were so genuinely interested, caring, nurturing. You gave me such a sense of confidence that I could do anything, that I could be anything. How many parents give that to their children? You and Dad loved each other so completely, so authentically up until the day he died. I had never seen you cry once. Not once in my entire life! But you wailed when Dad was dying in your arms, and I didn't think you would ever stop crying. It was well over a year before that ended, and sometimes I thought you wouldn't be able to get through it — but you did. And you were always there for us — Cindy, me, dad — you built such a loving family.

"If you mean in the greater sense, could you have contributed to more people in larger ways? Yes, I suppose you could have. I always knew, and we talked about this, you would've made an amazing nurse. But, in your experience, that career wasn't an option. The education wasn't available for you and... it really wasn't something you yearned for. But we just all knew you would've been great at it. Mom, you saved two people's lives! Who can claim this? You saved Dad's life with CPR, and again you saved a perfect stranger in a restaurant until the ambulance got there. You kept them both alive.

"I mean, that's just who you were and that's just what you did: care for people, love people, nurture people, take care of people. Never to the exclusion of yourself, seemingly, but because it gave you joy, value and meaning. So, when you say that you didn't make much of your life, I find it to be heartbreaking and gut-wrenching. That you would exit this world with the thought that you didn't make an enormous impact or create a legacy that I will be carrying out from this point forward...."

That was the moment when I decided no one should ever feel that way. No one! And certainly not somebody's mother. I invite you to do your work now. There's no need for you to feel this way when your time for reflection comes.

> This book is your roadmap to help you live your life with full passion and joy. Every day. By aligning your Purpose with your Passion and Profit.

One caveat: once you walk into your purpose, you must *never* look back with regret. You may want to question why you hadn't discovered this path sooner. But, in fact, everything has led you to this moment; just as it was designed to do. Nothing has gone to waste — not time, not trials, not unfulfilled dreams. On this guided journey you will see how everything in your life has had a purpose and you will not need to wish that one moment of your life had been different.

"If we were to become all we are truly capable of, we would quite literally astound ourselves."

— THOMAS EDISON

What a Life of Purpose Is Like

What if you woke up every day eager to start your day? Approaching each day with curiosity and child-like wonder, with the confidence of knowing you are indeed here for a reason? Recognizing the miracle of you even being here triggering deep appreciation and gratitude, allowing you to release the weight of judgment (of yourself and others) and embrace the lightness of humility and joy?

AND what if you audaciously incorporated this into how you go about making a living? Not only by doing what you love but also by embracing being who you are?

And what if the outcome of this was to magnetize people, the "right" people that can truly value and appreciate you, into your life as a result? And what if as a result of that you were able to positively impact those very same people's lives along the way?

I'm writing this book for the purpose of not only telling you, YOU CAN, but also showing you how! I call this **creating demand for your brand... from the inside out.**

Create Demand For Your Brand takes you on a journey from the inside out, resulting in a joy-filled life that attracts others to it, bringing external success. This book will illuminate the intersection of your purpose and your brand and how you can align both to produce genuine fulfillment. This alignment is what (referencing familiar expressions) allows you to "live in the zone," "go with the flow," experience the "law of attraction," to "do what you love and the money will follow," to be who you are in all that you do and attract success like a magnet.

This is probably a good time to share two things with you:

1. I'm not a fan of "motivational" anything. I am passionate about "inspirational" everything: finding *the* way to uniquely inspire myself, and helping others to find their unique ways to best inspire themselves.
2. I believe in pragmatism. What's the point of learning something valuable if you can't (or don't) utilize it?

This book is designed, first, to help you recognize and then understand the uniqueness within yourself. Next, to show you how to fully leverage and build upon that to create demand for yourself as a result. (In fact, we will discuss and make available discovery tools I use daily as part of my Masterclass Coaching work with clients. Many of these tools you can access for free simply by going to **Skilset.com/QuickStartToolkit**.)

Maybe you are looking for a mentor or maybe you want to mentor others; perhaps you're ready for a "Sherpa" who can guide you or a collaborator who can provide you the tools to identify your purpose and activate it. If that's the case, this book is for you!

One more thing I learned from my mom: life is too short. There is a finite amount of time. There are only so many hours in the day, day's in the year, and years in our life.

I don't know anyone who tells me they have too much time on their hands. So I'll ask you: how much more "doing" can you do?

If you're at the point where you know you can't DO any more than what you already are and there are no more hours to access, then you're ready to re-examine not just what you are doing but *how* you are doing it. As you know, it's not about working harder, it's about working smarter — which I submit means working *purposefully*.

It's also possible you are just starting your journey. You may be in school, just graduating, starting out in the workforce, becoming an entrepreneur, or a new manager. In that case, you may know you want to "make things count" from the get-go. If that's you, then you too are ready to explore the following pages. In fact, it's perfect timing for you! There's no need to stumble or fumble for the next 20 years to learn how to do this; you can climb atop my shoulders and those of the thousands I've worked with before you.

When is the right time for someone – for *you* – to stop "doing" and start "being"?

RIGHT NOW!

And that can happen. You just need to be willing to see things differently.

"People who wonder whether the glass is half empty or half full miss the point; the glass is refillable."

— ANONYMOUS

2

The Power of Purpose

ONE OF THE KEY QUESTIONS I am asked time and again is, "Why is it so difficult for people to identify their purpose?" I have concluded after thousands of such interactions there are three key reasons:

1. We are looking in the wrong direction — outside rather than within.
2. It appears it is just "who we are" — so much so that we often don't even see it.
3. We don't seem to value it — even if we do recognize it.

The answer to identifying our purpose lies in an internal journey of discovery.

Further, I have concluded that it is meant to be this way. It is our destiny for the journey of finding our purpose to be unnatural, uneasy, challenging. It needs to be a choice for conscious living that drives us to rebel against our external vision tendencies and turn inward to discover what was there all along.

This is where our growth takes place. This is where we learn about ourselves. The external view is but the laboratory where we experience and play out what we are discovering (or, what we are simply reacting to when we are living an unconscious life — much like the ball in a pinball machine). And the more challenging the journey within, the more conviction we experience when we make the discovery.

> This book is designed to help you find your purpose and discover how to integrate it in your everyday life and work life, so that you can reach your full potential, realize deep fulfillment and attract greater wealth and joy in the process.

Discovering our life purpose is about conscious living — living by design rather than by default. It's not about where we were born, what our parents wanted or what we were told we deserve. Instead, it's about self-discovery, and having the courage to be all we were intended to become. And since we do what we do for a living eight-plus hours a day, it's about aligning what we *do* with who we *are*, truly, authentically and deeply. When who we are is reflected in what we do, we not only experience more congruency within ourselves — we demonstrate that authenticity to the outside world. This often translates into inspiration.

Congruency Is Your Calling Card

In this day and age of transparency, of demanding authenticity and exposing inauthenticity, congruency is our calling card. It is no longer enough to "do a good job": it's about being an authentic person. When someone is going to work for your company, they search Glassdoor.com to see what is being said about your company. When you are applying to work for a company, the company does a search on you.

A company wants to know you are who you say you are, you are not a risk to the firm and you are a rational, reasonable, professional person. An individual wants to align with an organization that can truly appreciate who they are, where they can be free to express themselves at the office and outside of the office in a forthcoming manner.

Everyone isn't a right-fit for every situation — in work or in personal relationships. For you to live authentically and congruently, you need to know who you are and what's important to you.

> Identifying your purpose and letting that guide the choices you make – the choices that create your brand – will help you to effortlessly be your authentic self and attract others to you that are in complete alignment with you.

When you and your brand are authentic and congruent, you can let your brand work for you even while you're sleeping. You will be seen as the expert in your field, the go-to in your organization, a must-have on the team and a smart investment by others.

Working with people from every walk of life, from Senior Level Executives to Students, I have learned that we all yearn for one key thing: to know why we are here — our purpose. And if we are (seemingly) "lucky" enough to discover this, we can then look at how to integrate that purpose into our everyday lives. How do we get to live with passion? How do we get to do what makes our heart sing?

The fact is, it's not luck. And you can indeed discover your purpose and how to integrate it into your life. You can align your Purpose with your Passion and make it your source of Profit!

Sound like a tall order to you? Or does it sound like exactly what you are looking for? In either case, if you're saying, "Sign me up"... keep reading. This book's for you!

"Brand" Is a Way of Being

So, how is living a life of authenticity and congruency based on our own, individualized, inner-directed purpose linked to creating a personal "brand"?

"Brand" in this sense is *who you are known as in the world.* Apple has a brand. So does Microsoft. So does Tesla, General Electric, Wells Fargo and every other company or organization. And we each have a *personal* brand that defines us to others. Today everyone — yes, along with the Kardashians — accepts they are a brand. It's just undeniable. And while some brands can be associated with seemingly vapid fame, others can be associated with substance and value.

> It is vital that your personal "brand" reflect an authentic way of being. And authenticity is sustainable when it is based upon your purpose.

I recognize that today, unlike even 10 years ago, people are ready to consider their purpose and acknowledge the desire for knowing what theirs is. Not just for creating demand for their career, or for fame or solely for fortune, but for their own self-realization, fulfillment, filling a gnawing gap and gaining a North Star to guide their choices — how they live their life, how they share their life and what they do to create money, joy and true success.

This book is your roadmap to discover your authentic personal "brand" that will allow you to live a life filled with Purpose, Passion and Profit. Part 1 of this book is about Discovery. It will take you on a journey to *you* — recognizing and then understanding your Purpose. Part 2 is your roadmap. It will guide you on how to purposefully design your brand. When these two parts come together, your brand creates demand for you.

> The truth is, we are all a brand. The only question is whether you are a brand by design or by default.

The Paradox of the Path to Purpose

Look, it's natural to seek outside ourselves for the answer. In our most formative years we look to everyone else for answers, guidance, even our very survival. When we are children, our parents innocently drive us in the directions they understand, recognize and/or respect, based on their perceptions, their fears and their dreams. Our parents are "innocent" in that what they teach us is what they know (just as if you are or become a parent, you will teach your children what you know).

As children, we think our parents are all-knowing heroes, gods. They seem to know EVERYTHING! And for a child, they do. However, the reality is *we are responsible for our own lives*. Every choice we make either takes us closer toward our purpose, our vision, our goals, or farther away. And choice is the gift we are given to exercise.

You may be reading this book because you want to make better choices when it comes to life and work — choices that will lead you to greater fulfillment, a deeper sense of meaning for your life, more passion for what you do in the world, and yes, greater profit from your work.

The five steps described in this book were developed in hindsight. First I went through this process for myself, and then I coached several dozens of others through a similar journey. Step by step we explored, discovered and designed who they were and how they wanted to live their lives to the fullest. Along the way, I saw that breaking the process into smaller steps made it easier for people to reach their goals.

This book is a summation of the workshops and the private coaching that have taken place with thousands of people over the past 20 years. It also is a reflection of countless requests from those I've had the great pleasure to help guide so they could share what they have learned with those they care about. I'm humbled by the many requests to help them share it and honored to do so.

I, and the people in my workshops through the years, will attest that this is a priceless journey you are beginning. Let's get started!

PART TWO

Your Roadmap

3

Step One: Introspection — from the Inside Out

> *"Your visions will become clear only when you can look into your own heart. Who looks outside, dreams; who looks inside, awakes."*
>
> — CARL JUNG

NTROSPECTION IS ABOUT GETTING SO CLEAR on who you are that it consistently drives your focus and your passion. It gives you permission to begin to understand that not only is it okay to live your life's purpose as a way to create profit and a lifestyle, but it is what was intended in the first place.

When you are living in your purpose, you feel it. You feel energized. You feel passionate. You feel excited. You feel inspired. You feel driven. Or you may feel a yearning, a deep sense of wonder, or curiosity, until you figure it out. One way or another, you are stimulated by that purpose.

Discovering your purpose starts by trusting that however you got here in the world, whatever your belief system is... you are a miracle! Whether you put it down to science and the single sperm that found its way there fastest, or to your faith that leads you to believe that you have a divine reason for being, when you acknowledge that you are a miracle then you have to know that your purpose has already been put inside of you. All you are meant to do is allow it to be, to exist, to flourish.

However, you must have the courage to silence the inner voice of judgment that can derail your sense of purpose. That voice may be based on your parents' beliefs (which you've adopted) and the impact of societal norms where you live in the world or the time in which you are living. You must learn to suspend that internal voice and move into a place of trust and faith that your purpose is within you — whether you're able to see it easily, or it takes immense struggle and you have to dig deep (which, by the way, it does for most of us).

That is part of the journey. If finding your purpose were easy, there would be no point. Yet if you'll trust and respect the struggle and let it guide you, you will arrive at your purpose. As did these recognizable people:

- A beautiful heiress from a wealthy family was named Agnes Bojaxhiu. She discovered her purpose and evolved to become Mother Teresa.
- A mischievous schoolboy, cited to be "stupid, restless and a slow learner who asks too many questions" followed his purpose and illuminated the world — literally. He is Thomas Edison.
- A shy and unpopular loner brought up in terribly poor and primarily black neighborhoods and housing projects landed his first real job as a truck driver for the Crown Electric Company. He became recognized as Elvis Presley. (One might argue that he discovered his

talent but never aligned his purpose with his passion and profit. Thus an enormously talented man led a turbulent life with a tragic ending.)

Authentic Versus Synthetic Purpose

When you begin this search, you may discover that you have been living what I'll call a "synthetic" purpose: one that is manufactured by someone else's vision or goal for you. Perhaps you realize that it was someone else's purpose you've been living — maybe your parents, your spouse, or social pressures, or…. (You can likely finish that thought with your own story.)

Often this occurs because you didn't trust yourself; you didn't see yourself as a miracle. Maybe you didn't have the courage or the understanding to venture inside to learn what your purpose is. Perhaps you never asked yourself why you are here, and since you didn't know, you settled. Perhaps you didn't have a clear vision for yourself so you listened to someone else's ideas. Or perhaps your self-doubt didn't let you take responsibility for your choices.

This realization may show up as a mid-life crisis, or an end of career "aha" moment. If you're fortunate, it may be something you recognize in your school years or when someone hands you this book. When I'm working with teenagers or young adults, in university in particular, their families have typically put them through some level of costly education to help them find a way to make a life for themselves and become independent beings. Oftentimes they are juniors or graduating seniors, yet they "still don't know what they want to do" — and they worry that they don't know. This is when they make a choice to default to imitating what their parents are doing or what their parents have suggested they should do. Thus they abdicate responsibility for their own life, or for living their life's purpose and fulfilling their full potential.

But how can somebody else possibly know what your purpose is? Most people don't even know what their *own* is — how could they possibly define yours?

It's fascinating to have those conversations with young adults because they often share that they are struggling with a direction they are defaulting to rather than designing (and will likely follow that direction by adopting a career path that isn't their own). Intuitively they know that they are not doing what they want to do, but they aren't sure what "that" is. Their unknowing isn't likely because of what they think it is — i.e., they don't have life experience, they don't know what it's like to live in that profession, they don't know what the job is, and so on. In my experience, their discomfort with their choice (or their lack of assuredness about someone's choice they are adopting) comes from an inner voice that they may or may not be familiar with yet. That voice is talking to them, but they don't yet know how to hear. What they are experiencing is incongruence with their internal self.

This is why understanding one's self and sitting quietly — whether that's in meditation or prayer or self-reflection of some kind — is so important. It's essential that you quiet your mind to get in touch with the inner voice that knows the absolute truth about what your purpose is.

Am I in Alignment with My Purpose?

How do you know when you are not living your authentic purpose? It's easy to recognize: you are not sustainably energized or excited. You lack passion. You find you are talking yourself out of bed in the morning to go do what you are to do. These are clues that you are not living your life's purpose.

Fortunately, I have put decades of discovery and experience into helping people discover their purpose, and I'm happy to share with you some of the tools and processes that I tap into or have developed through my own internal journey as well as in our interactive workshops and retreats.

One such tool reveals your *motivators*, or the driving forces of your behavior. It's an assessment that asks you a series of questions, and then you receive a report that helps you understand what really drives you. (If you would like more information about taking the assessment yourself, go to **Skilset.com/motivators**.) Your motivators essentially tell you why you do what you do. They are not dependent upon where you were born in the world, what family you did or did not belong to, or where you work. Instead, they have to do with who you are as a unique human being and what truly drives you.

There are six core motivators. I can summarize them as follows.

- Theoretical: a love for learning
- Utilitarian: a pragmatic focus and practical application
- Aesthetic: an internal drive for self-actualization
- Social: a "cause" orientation — empathetic toward others' pain / suffering
- Individualistic: a desire to control your own destiny and that of others
- Traditional: operating with a strong set of guiding principles and beliefs

While all six motivators are present in everyone, each person has two key drivers that are more compelling than the other four. My two key drivers happen to be *Utilitarian* and *Aesthetic*.

These drivers illuminate why I do what I do, which is to help people align their purpose, passion and profit.

As an *Aesthetic* focused on self-actualization, I am on a quest to be the best I can be. I know that in order for me to fulfill my potential to the fullest, I need to keep journeying, discovering, and becoming all that I can.

I am also *Utilitarian*. I seek and learn about myself, and then I utilize the information, develop my own tools and discoveries, put them into a process and turn it into a pragmatic business offering.

With these as my top two drivers, I live my life everyday learning, growing, putting what I learn into an applicable process and then teaching it to others so they can reach their full potential (and getting paid to do so). I can't say that I designed it that way up front, although I could have if I had understood about key drivers then. It organically occurred because of how I think due to my Aesthetic and Utilitarian drivers. And it's also because of my drive to self-reflect that I came to understand this many years later.

Today whenever I work with people, I start them off with discovery tools right from the beginning. Discovering *your* key drivers will help you move forward with informed grace and speed. (To learn more about what truly drives you and obtain your personal assessment at a significant discount — available to purchasers of this book — go to **Skilset.com/motivators**.)

Pragmatic Application: Key Drivers in Action

I was coaching a client recently whose story shows how purpose, passion, and profit come to life when you understand your drivers. Here's Cristiana's background:

- She is relatively new to managing, with six direct reports in a professional services firm.
- Her mother is very ill.
- She's in a relationship where she has a live-in teenaged stepchild.
- Her behavioral style is such that she innately has very high standards — a perfectionist by nature.
- She has a lot of responsibility.
- She is hard on herself.

She told me that she wanted coaching because she was struggling with helping a couple of the people within her team. Her two key drivers are *Theoretical* (she has a love of learning) and *Individualistic* (she strives to be in control of her own destiny and the destiny of others — she innately has a drive to be a leader).

We began by re-visiting a prior discussion around the distinction between managing and leading. She said that while she "used to take pride in prescribing to her team" (a.k.a. managing or directing them), now she sees leadership as "her ability to help someone else discover for themselves; helping to develop their conscious critical thinking." We then discussed the art and skill of learning to ask questions in order to help others *discover and learn new things* (tapping into her Theoretical driver), because asking versus telling is actively developing rather than managing.

Next, we discussed the distinction between being a leader and leadership (linking to her Individualistic driver). She could see that leadership was a title: something that is bestowed; something that signals to others who is in charge. And she could also see that being a leader is a practice, a way of being. It's a *behavior*, not a title. And when done well, with consistency and authenticity, it will attract people who want to be a part of the leader's team.

Then we discussed what was going on with her personally — the pressures of personal life and work life in combination. As she described it, "When I'm overwhelmed it feels like the walls are closing in; like I have no choices; like suffocating." I reminded her that to be authentic, credible, trustworthy leaders, people who lead others must also model leading *themselves*. We began to look at how she could lead herself just as she leads her team. What questions could she ask of herself to develop herself into a better leader?

I reminded her that she could best tie these questions to her own drivers. When we know our drivers, we have the ability to leverage them, to tap into them, to use them to fuel and energize us. So she created two questions to help keep her from feeling overwhelmed and without choices.

Tying into her Theoretical motivator to help keep her inspired, independently, from the inside out (which will help her stay on task) her first question is: *"What have I learned today?"*

Every obstacle, every challenge is a learning and growth opportunity, I reminded her. "Life" will happen during any given day; the question is, how will you choose to look at it?

Her second question is: *"What have I taught of value to someone today?"*

As a leader committed to developing others (tying into her Individualistic motivator), I suggested that she look for the opportunity to guide and develop her team. Then she could acknowledge the behaviors she had put in place and let them energize her.

When she came up with those two questions, she instantly shifted and with genuine relief and excitement exclaimed, "YES! If I listen to a podcast when I'm down, I move from feeling limited to seeing choices. If I see something new, I think, 'If this is possible for them, it is also a possibility for me.' By learning something new I see choices, and I feel better." (This matches with her Theoretical driver.)

"And I don't want to be a manager who tells people what to do or just pushes paper. I want to help them." She choked up and added, "Not just as a manager, but as a human being, I want to help people." (This connects to her Individualistic motivator: she wants to lead/influence/impact others.)

We then found a new phrase for her. Instead of a "manager," she decided to call herself a "practitioner of leadership." She said that felt like active learning (her Theoretical motivator) and seemed fluid and airy as opposed to static and stifling.

Finally, we added a question she can ask herself each morning to stay on track. Her third question is: *How will I be a practitioner of leadership today?*

This starts her day off consciously, seeking opportunities to be her best, to help others, to live in her purpose with energy and enthusiasm.

The key to the success of this coaching session is my understanding of what her motivators are so I know what is important *to her*, what drives her *at her core*. I can then tailor questions and guide discussion to develop her specifically and uniquely. She is guided to make self-discovery from the Inside

Out. She can recognize her uniqueness and be reminded how to lead herself. She can take responsibility for her feeling of overwhelm so she doesn't feel suffocated and like she has no choices. Rather, she can get herself in alignment with her fulfilling desire to lead and learn, and in the process feel better about herself by living in alignment with who she is.

For her company, she is becoming a stronger leader. For her team, she is helping them to advance. Best of all, *how* she does it is with genuine passion, based upon who she is and how she is driven.

This process would, *and should*, be entirely different for someone with different drivers.

The Inside Out Formula™

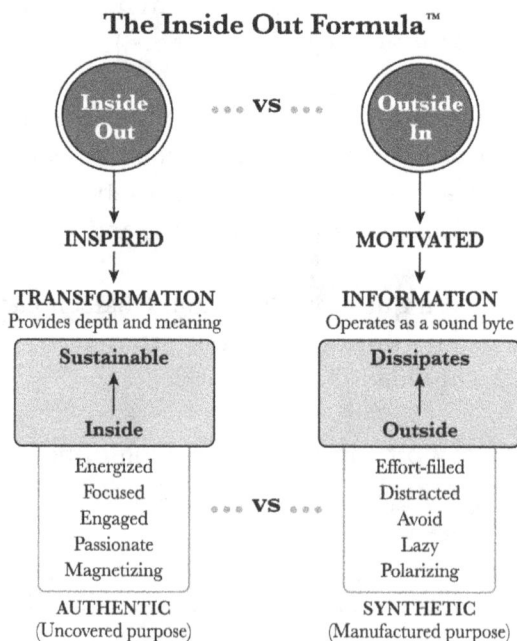

Inside Out	...VS...	Outside In
INSPIRED		MOTIVATED
TRANSFORMATION		INFORMATION
Provides depth and meaning		Operates as a sound byte
Sustainable		Dissipates
Inside		Outside
Energized		Effort-filled
Focused		Distracted
Engaged ...VS...		Avoid
Passionate		Lazy
Magnetizing		Polarizing
AUTHENTIC		SYNTHETIC
(Uncovered purpose)		(Manufactured purpose)

Aligning your purpose and your passion can only come through discovery from the inside out. This is why this book isn't light and fluffy with the intention to simply motivate. Motivation that occurs from the outside in wears thin, wears off. It's often filled with kitschy sound bytes but little substance. What I'm interested in is *transformation* — guiding internal discoveries that illuminate and cultivate who we are. This is sustainable because it energizes us, empowers us, exploits our passions and renders us a magnetizing force drawing our audiences to us.

> The distinction is moving from Outside In to Inside Out.

A Pivotal Portal to Self

One of the pivotal portals or doorways you have to walk through to know yourself and align your purpose with your passion and profit is what I call Introspection. It is the first step of the five-step process for creating demand for your brand. It is what informs and guides the next four steps.

Let me take you through the steps for a moment to set the stage.

Step One: Introspection — From the Inside Out

Step Two: Differentiation — Why You?

Step Three: Your Unique Message

Step Four: Creating Brand Buzz — Let Your Purpose Guide You

Step Five: Maintenance — Aligning Your Choices (this sounds a bit boring and dull, but it's actually *very* exciting)

Unfortunately, most people gravitate toward starting somewhere other than Introspection. They start with Step Two or Three or Four (particularly with all the social media tools available now) without uncovering what is revealed in Step One. Yet the work in Step One makes all the following steps easy to design authentically and naturally, instead of struggling to manufacture something synthetic and forced.

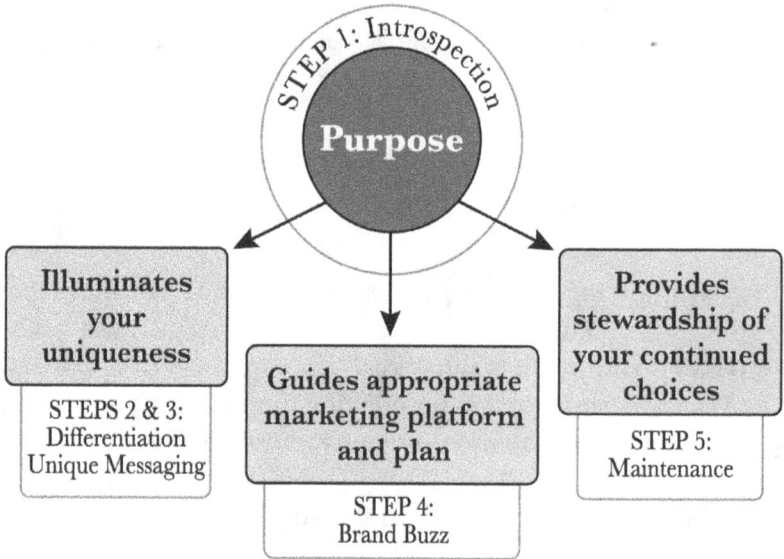

STEP 1: Introspection

Purpose

Illuminates your uniqueness

STEPS 2 & 3:
Differentiation
Unique Messaging

Guides appropriate marketing platform and plan

STEP 4:
Brand Buzz

Provides stewardship of your continued choices

STEP 5:
Maintenance

There are a couple of reasons people generally want to skip over this first step: (1) it may seem like too much work, and (2) it is unfamiliar and perhaps uncomfortable to go inside. I would suggest it is uncomfortable precisely *because* it is unfamiliar. But like anything else, once you exercise courage to move forward, it isn't as scary as you anticipated.

> You were designed for this journey of self-discovery. And it was intended to call upon some level of courage. This is what makes it worthwhile, and what helps us appreciate what we discover.

Think of it as your own personal treasure hunt — and in reality, it is worth more than gold, because it is the gateway to the fulfillment that comes from aligning what you do with who you are. When that occurs, riches follow. People are attracted to you — magnetized, in fact. Subconsciously they know you have something they want, because purpose is something each of us yearns for, whether we are conscious of it or not.

Getting Started

The good news here is you have plenty of material to work with. You can start by doing a self-audit — and there is no one "right" way to do so. Do it in whatever way feels energizing to you. Depending on what drives you, your way may be something that is creative (like a mind map), or fun (like a metaphor), or more structured and pragmatic (like a framework).

There are certain categories of thought that will set you on the right track to discovery.

On the next two pages, you'll find an example of how you might frame your audit, and a blank template for you to use in Step One of your own brand development. Or you can download a blank PDF at **Skilset.com/BrandSelfAudit**.

Once you've completed the self-audit, we can then identify your key discoveries. Which events and items do you recognize as the ones that truly shaped you in some way — they illuminated what you find energizing, what you realized you are capable of, drawn to, or what you did because of someone else versus what you wanted to do? These are the clues that lead you straight to your purpose.

Brand Self Audit
Step 1: Introspection

PASSION	PERSONALITY	TALENTS	DEFINING MOMENTS	FAMILY/CULTURE	EXPERIENCES	WORKLIFE	EDUCATION
Self-discovering	Direct	Listening	8 years old - advising	Midwest values	Fire walk	Sales - Top 2% before 30	UCLA
Inspiring	Confident	Articulating	Moment I met my husband	Married 29 years	First speaking - 800 people	Only non-owner on Board	Summit Organization
Thoughtful celebrations	Soul-searcher	Communication	Japanese Tour to U.S. for IndiBrand™	Traditional	25 trips to Portugal	Author	DISC Certified
Architectural design	Risk taker	Strategic	Pre-law to an unknown	Encouraging	Piloting a helicopter	Entrepreneur	NSA Certification
Imagination	Curious	Creative	Observing Father's death	Work ethic	Skydiving with son	Innovator of IndiBrand™ CHOICE™	Seminars
CANI	Courageous	Insightful	Conversation with dying mother	Dependable	TEDx Coaching	Consultant/coach to Fortune 500's	Ongoing...
Brand Purpose	Brand Expression	Brand Differentiation	Influencers Brand Story	Influencers Brand Story	Brand Muscle	Brand Application	Brand Tools

SKILSET COMMUNICATIONS, INC.
Create Demand For Your Brand

Michele Lando
Aligning Purpose, Passion, & Profit

Brand Self Audit
Step 1: Introspection

PASSION	PERSONALITY	TALENTS	DEFINING MOMENTS	FAMILY/CULTURE	EXPERIENCES	WORKLIFE	EDUCATION
Brand Purpose	Brand Expression	Brand Differentiation	Influencers Brand Story	Influencers Brand Story	Brand Muscle	Brand Application	Brand Tools

There is a reason why one person is drawn to something, is energized by it, fueled by it, and another isn't at all. It is the internal magnetic pull toward our purpose.

We can also categorize your insights to help you design your brand. What are the items that contribute to your differentiation (Step Two), or help you craft your unique message to attract your audience (Step Three)? What stories and/or vehicles make sense for you to integrate when creating brand buzz (Step Four)?

What you will gain by this exercise are a set of markers that define what truly makes you uniquely you. These markers become the roadmap to guide your awareness of self and your understanding of what you bring to the party. You can use this roadmap to align yourself in an authentic and organic way when engaging with your audiences.

This is the first step in aligning your Purpose, Passion and Profit. Congratulations on being committed to getting started!

4

Step Two: Differentiation — Why You?

"Do your work with your whole heart and you will succeed — there is so little competition."

— ELBERT HUBBARD

WHEN YOU ARE NOT ALIGNED WITH YOUR PURPOSE your job feels like "work." When you align what you do with who you are, work becomes a vehicle to live your passion. And this differentiates you.

Many people want to get out there and start "branding" or promoting themselves before they have given real thought to what they want their brand to be. However, continually creating demand for your brand requires more than just being known. "Being known" may turn you into a trend or make you interesting for a time, but if you want to create ongoing demand, you must build a *sustainable* brand — and that requires thought and strategy. You must determine who and what you want to be known for or known as in the marketplace.

> You must know what differentiates you and your brand from everyone else.

In companies, this differentiation is called a UVP, or Unique Value Proposition. With individuals, it's often referred to as your USP, or Unique Selling Proposition. Regardless of the nomenclature, in both instances it is a focused examination of "why you": what separates you from your competition — the factors that make you unique and desirable. Ultimately, your differentiation will be based on the *value* you create for your audience, which is composed of the clients, customers, and business associates you work with or serve.

In Step One you looked at the fundamentals of who you are, where you came from, where you are going, how you want to get there, and what you consider the defining qualities that make you, you. In Step Two you will switch gears from Introspection, or looking from the *Inside Out*, to tapping into your audience and seeing yourself from the *Outside In*, so you can discover the value you create for others.

> And how will you know what your audience believes your value to be? Ask them!

One of the most powerful tools that we use in our workshops is called "Unique Attributes," adapted from Dan Sullivan's Strategic Coach® program. The "Unique Attributes" exercise provides clues that help you determine the positive characteristics and traits people associate with you. Workshop attendees send requests to between five and ten people whom they trust and respect, asking them to describe the unique attributes, talents, affinities, and characteristics they attribute to the attendee. Then, in the workshop, each person reads the descriptions they received.

It is so rewarding for people to see how others view, appreciate, and respect them. It's especially meaningful because it isn't just anyone they are hearing it from: these descriptions come from people they know and hold in high regard. It's very common for powerful grown men and women to well up with tears of humility while reading how others have described them. It is an illuminating, touching and, frequently, life-changing experience.

(If you'd like to do the same exercise yourself, I've made the Unique Attributes tool available for you. To get your free tool, go to **Skilset.com/UniqueAttributes**.)

This exercise is so powerful because most of us simply don't recognize what makes us unique and special — it is so much a part of who we are that we just don't see it. And if by chance, we do take the time to notice what makes us unique and special, we likely won't value it because we didn't do anything to earn it. We didn't have to work for our uniqueness; it's just part of us. It's like blinking: can you imagine giving yourself a pat on the back and saying, "Good job! You've been doing some amazing blinking today"?

Yet the qualities we didn't work for, that just "showed up," are incredibly valuable! In fact, those qualities are intrinsically linked to your purpose. They are the essence of the miracle that you are, revealed in a tangible, visible expression!

Here are a few summarized illustrations of the kinds of feedback people receive from the "Unique Attributes" exercise. Notice how different the feedback is from one person to another. The range shows you how uniqueness begins to emerge in each individual. And these contribute significantly to the building blocks for each person's brand. (Of course, we take this discovery to a whole other level in our workshops, where we can have a conversation about these qualities in real time.)

**Example 1: Avi Cohen, Managing Director,
Fortune 50 Financial Services Company**

- Hard worker
- Desire to do the right thing
- Takes ownership; doesn't let others do the analysis
- Anticipates roadblocks
- Thinks several steps ahead
- Loyal
- Confident
- Persevering
- Affable
- Won't take no for an answer
- Passionate
- When you commit to something, you are all in

You will have the opportunity to see how Avi's characteristics are used in his brand messaging in Step Three.

Example 2: Robert Weiner, Vice President, Major and Planned Gifts, Children's Hospital Los Angeles Foundation

- Compassionate
- People person
- Immediately likable
- Inspires trust
- A source of information
- Articulate communicator
- Organized
- Respectful
- Sincere
- Diplomatic
- Honorable
- Committed to making the world a better place
- Special sense of humor
- Incredible knack for remembering what you read or hear
- Patient
- Focused
- Doesn't freak out
- Enthusiastic
- Athletic
- Helpful

Example 3: Carol Araki, Sr. Vice President, Operations, a Global Commercial Real Estate and Investment Company

- Consistent
- Diligent
- Ability to analyze — a project, system, problem
- Impartial assessment
- Inclusive strategist
- Tireless
- Always improving knowledge base
- Honest
- Frank/blunt
- Big picture
- Visit another's perspective
- Follow up, follow up, and follow up
- Identify the heartbeat of a situation
- Refocus a group
- "Can do" person
- Sound logic and relevant examples
- Not afraid to question
- Listens intently
- Personable
- Insatiable passion for her work
- Sustains highest standards
- Infectious laugh
- Pragmatic
- Quick thinker
- Considerate, caring
- Good writer
- Lover of culinary arts

Example 4: Victoria Hoffman, Senior Sales Director, Mary Kay Cosmetics

- Great organizational skills
- Isolates salient ideas from big picture
- Very good listener
- Analytical
- Self-disciplined
- Compassionate (but not in a sentimental way)
- Committed and loyal
- Nurturing
- Classy
- Ethical
- Likeable
- Business savvy
- Personal drive
- Successful

**Example 5: Lee Jackman, Vice President,
Doheny Eye Institute (Nonprofit)**

- Ready ahead of time
- Great planner
- Diligent
- Stays on task
- Great empathy and generosity
- Direct
- Creative
- Intellectually curious
- Self-reflection, introspection
- Balanced perspective
- Passionate
- Principled
- Fun-loving
- Socially conscious
- Gregarious
- Proud
- High standards
- Great citizen
- Fantastic parent
- Part of something truly bigger than life itself
- Intuitive
- Eager to mentor
- Multi-tasker
- Persuasive
- Charismatic
- In charge
- Likes structure
- Superb learner/listener
- Excellent presence
- Great networker
- Creative — music, writing

By now you are probably wondering what your colleagues, clients, contacts value about *you*. If so, go to **Skilset.com/UniqueAttributes** to access the invitation you can send to them so you can find out.

Two Ways to Differentiate Your Brand

As I've said before, you must first be clear on who you are (introspection) and what makes you unique (differentiation/why you). Only then can you see how to make this truly valuable and meaningful to your audience.

There are multiple layers to this process, and while we cover it extensively in our webinars, workshops and retreats, I can highlight a few elements here to help you understand that even within your particular audience, people are not all the same.

#1: Brand Triggers Emotion

All brands have an emotional component to them. In fact, you elicit an emotion whenever you engage with others. It might be positive, it might be negative, or it might be neutral.

- If it's *positive*, they have a good feeling about you, or they are intrigued, or they want more.
- If it's *negative*, they have a bad feeling about you. They are deterred, or put off, or depending on how strong the negative reaction, they may be repelled.
- If it's *neutral*, you haven't struck a chord one way or the other. They may not care about you; they may not even remember you.

Clearly a positive connection is better than a negative one. But which is better: a negative emotion or a neutral one? While I wouldn't encourage going for a negative emotional response intentionally, I would say it might be preferred over a neutral one. Why? This is where the only lesson I can recall from my undergraduate physics course comes into play: *For every action, there is an equal and opposite reaction.*

Think about someone you strongly disagreed with, or you had no respect for, and then you changed your mind. Perhaps you learned they didn't do what you thought they did, and you had falsely judged them. Or you learned *why* they did something or said something, and it changed your perception of them completely. It's that "completely" part that makes the negative more desirable.

Let's say that you had strong negative feelings about someone — call that a -10. But then you realize you misjudged them and you feel terrible about it. Or you discover why they did something and you feel empathy for them. When you shift your perspective, you often move in direct proportion from -10 to +10.

Why is this important? If someone feels strongly negative about you, there's a greater opportunity to have this person become a convert, a champion of you — or what we call your Brand Ambassador!

Here's the lesson: if you mess up, clean it up to the best of your ability. If you do, you will likely transform some "haters" into "fans."

#2: Facts Tell, Stories Sell

Neutral brand associations often render you unmemorable. This is where *story* becomes so valuable. We've been trained to listen to and repeat stories since we heard our first nursery rhymes. For example, where did Jack and Jill go? Why? And then what happened? (And that story was told to you how many years ago?) When someone tells you a story, you are more likely to remember the person and the point he or she made. If the story is meaningful enough, you're even likely to re-tell the story.

When I teach this concept in a workshop, I will say, "Remember these five words: bugle, monkey, tree, ship, skateboard." About 30 minutes later, I'll ask, "Who can tell me the five words I asked you to remember?" You can probably guess how few people come up with the words. It's not easy because the words make no "sense."

But then I say, "What if I told you a fun story about an island in the Caribbean where cruise ships have been stopping for many years, where families get to watch the monkeys play on the island? And where kids have left toys behind, including a bugle and a skateboard? The monkeys learned to skateboard and they love it. In fact, they climb a tree to scout daily to see if a cruise ship coming. If so, they sound the bugle so the others can hide the toys to keep the kids from taking them!"

Could you see the monkeys? Hear the bugle? Could you recall the five words more easily by recalling the story? Of course!

Would you want to visit that island? (If being around playful monkeys sounds like fun to you, you would. Of course, "fun" may look altogether different to someone else. My cousin Rose certainly wouldn't call that fun; when she visited Costa Rica, she wanted to get as far away from the monkeys as possible.)

Maybe the visual of this story made you smile or even chuckle. Maybe it seemed silly and you scoffed. Either way, it likely didn't leave you neutral. And it certainly made the "facts" of the island experience more memorable.

There's data, and then there's relevance. There are facts, and then there's illumination. Whenever possible, you want to turn your knowledge, your expertise, into a story — ideally, one that is attractive to more of the same audience you want to attract. Why? Because people aren't buying your product / service / or even you, based on facts. ***People buy based on emotion.***

For example, if I buy an iPhone, I may feel:

- excited by the design,
- a sense of belonging / being part of an elite community,
- secure knowing that I've purchased reliability and a strong customer support system, etc.

There are other phones (like Androids) that offer the same size, the same storage capacity, the same apps, and so on. But I'm not buying strictly on the data points of the phone. I'm buying the *emotions* I feel when I buy an iPhone. The same is true if I engage you or your services. I'm not buying the service: I'm buying what I believe your service will make me feel like.

The emotion that you strive to fulfill for your audience will vary depending on the product or service that you offer. Here are a few examples of businesses / services and the emotions they can potentially create.

Service	Emotion
Beauty treatment	Excited
Insurance	Security
Educational degree	Hope
Massage	Nurtured
Island hopping with monkeys	Fun

Question: What is the key emotion you want to create in the minds of your clients and customers?

When we talk about the classical understanding of brands, we work toward having our brand be associated with one word, ideally one emotion, such as:

Abe Lincoln = Honesty

Volvo = Safety

Michele Lando = Transformation

You = _____ (fill in the blank)

What key emotion do you want associated with you and your brand? You might want to look back over the list of key attributes, talents, affinities, and characteristics that other people attribute to you, and choose one you feel speaks most powerfully to the audience for you and your product or service. Do you want to inspire? Lead? Nurture? Support? Are you passionate? Analytical? Precise? Organized? Creative? Trustworthy? Articulate? A teambuilder? A communicator? Committed? Altruistic?

Once you have identified your word, the next step in branding yourself is to hone in on your *unique message*, as you'll see in Chapter 5.

5

Step Three: Your Unique Message

A NOTHER CRITICAL ELEMENT OF YOUR BRAND is your message. The first key objective is to *help people readily understand what you are offering*. To do this means you want to keep it simple and clear.

Your unique message should answer three questions:
(1) What do you do?
(2) Who do you do it for?
(3) And why should they care?

For example, my unique message is:

(1) I guide (2) companies and their individuals (3) to reach unimaginable outcomes.

You can also provide context — "how" in this case:

(1) I guide (2) companies and their individuals
(3) to reach unimaginable outcomes
by aligning their Purpose, Passion and Profit.

Many times when focusing in on developing their brand, people will start with Step Three. They may start by "packaging" themselves — whether in an introduction at a networking event, or promoting themselves in marketing materials, or with a speaking bio, on LinkedIn, or on a resume. But very often they find themselves struggling with what should be a relatively simple task. After all, how hard can it be to tell others who we are and what we do?

There's a problem, however: getting clarity around expressing or "packaging" ourselves is often like trying to do surgery on ourselves. We can see someone else clearly, but we see ourselves in multiple layers. We know too much about ourselves, in a sense, and this tends to complicate our thinking. What's worse, often we are trying to "sound our best" in our descriptions of ourselves — said another way, we're trying to impress.

The interesting aspect here is we are actually trying to impress *ourselves* first: to convince ourselves that we are worthy, valuable, and different in some way. This is why Step One: Introspection is critical. We have to take the time to be so clear on who we are that we actually *believe* what we say about ourselves. That way, our unique message will not be just external marketing "hype": instead, it will reflect the fact that we believe in ourselves, we are confident, and we are comfortable with who and what we say we are.

Rather than promoting ourselves by talking, we need to discover the truth by listening. Before "packaging" ourselves with a unique message, we need to (1) listen to ourselves and the people we interact with (colleagues and clients) and (2) reflect on what we have heard.

Once we arrive at this place by going through Steps One and Two, Introspection and Differentiation, we can stop focusing on ourselves and instead focus on how to make these discoveries meaningful for our audience.

> This is the second key to successful messaging: it's about crafting your message from your Customer's Point of View.

It's really very simple. If you are writing the check to yourself, you can say whatever you like however you like. But if you are looking for someone *else* to assign value to you, pay you, or write a check to you, then you need to know what they care about and message what you genuinely have to offer... from THEIR point of view!

Tying It All Together from Purpose through Step Three

Here are some illustrations of different people in the financial services industry messaging to their audiences in unique ways for different authentic reasons. Let's start with Avi, who is a managing director of a Fortune 50 financial services company. Avi attended one of our branding workshops, and as he discovered his purpose and went through Steps One and Two, Introspection and Differentiation, he came up with this statement as his core branding message.

Avi's Core Message: I make sure others don't have financial struggles.

The Unique Attributes Feedback Avi received prior to the workshop session allowed us to craft his message. It is shown below in abbreviated format. It included the essence of these traits:

- Hard worker
- Organized
- Conscientious
- Desire to do the right thing
- Passionate
- Client advocate
- Perseverance
- Puts in long hours
- Does the homework to understand your clients
- Gets into details
- Takes ownership; doesn't let others do the analysis
- Anticipates roadblocks
- Provides various solutions
- Thinks several steps ahead
- Able to clearly communicate
- Prompt on follow-through
- Acute understanding of your business
- Guides us to adjust with changing circumstances
- Determined — won't take no for an answer
- Loyal
- Confident
- Affable
- When you commit to something, you are all in

We used Avi's Unique Attributes Feedback to capture his authenticity and integrate it into his messaging. This aligns his message with the actual experience his customers will receive. We then incorporated some of his story into his Unique Message.

Incorporated into his Unique Message: I make sure others don't have financial struggles because....

(His Unique Message is based on his story — transparency and authenticity creates credibility.)

"My family came to America in 1987, fleeing Iran with no money in our pockets and not knowing the English language. I knew I never wanted my family, or anyone else's for that matter, to deal with financial struggles again.

"My clients' lives are constantly changing. I focus on being able to capture that change and be there to assist, to be forward thinking on their behalf — no surprises. I make sure they get where they need to go."

Validate and Verify Your Congruency

A powerful self-diagnostic tool featured in our workshops focuses on what truly motivates each of us. What is it that drives us from the deepest part of our being? As you read in Chapter 3, there are six key motivators. While they are universal, the order of the value we place on them is unique to each of us, and the depth to which we are driven by them will vary. However, it is always our top two drivers that truly motivate us. How those top two drivers show up in our lives can vary from one person to the next. In other words, it is possible for you to utilize these energizing drivers in a variety of industries and differing functional roles.

To live a life with your purpose, passion and profit in alignment, you will want to be sure that what differentiates you — how others see you as providing value — is in full alignment with your top two drivers. Otherwise, you will find yourself wondering why you're doing what you are doing — perhaps unhappy, or perhaps making a good livelihood but not connected to your energizing passion.

This is often where I get called in by senior people who are "successful" by all rights but who aren't feeling satiated, stimulated, or impassioned. They sense something is missing from their lives. They are looking for that deeper connection to themselves, to their purpose for being. They have a desire to experience true fulfillment and often to make a meaningful difference, whether inspired by thoughts of legacy (think Andrew Carnegie, Henry Ford, John Glenn, and Steve Jobs) or by impacting others (think Mother Theresa, Gandhi, John F. Kennedy, and Nelson Mandela).

Here's an illustration of Avi's top two drivers and how they integrate into his Unique Value Proposition/Differentiator and his Unique Message.

Example: Avi's Top Two Drivers

#1: Utilitarian

Innately, Avi is all about getting a return on investment. He will invest his resources (his time, talent, money, etc.) as long as he can see a direct outcome. This is true for himself and, because it is how he is driven, it is also how he services his clients. He is entirely practical and pragmatic. He is not going to steer his clients wrong. He's just not wired that way!

#2: Individualistic

This characteristic describes someone who is driven to have control over his own destiny and the destiny of others. This motivator will drive this person to ascend: to be the captain of the squad, leader of the group, owner of a company, President of the United States — and in Avi's case, to be a managing director who is in a position to guide his clients and assemble the right teams to support them.

Utilizing his Motivators Assessment, Avi is able to understand his own drivers. This allows him to gain confidence in recognizing his own authentic value and to create his unique message with the assurance that this is what truly differentiates him. (If you are wondering what your key drivers are, you can go to **Skilset.com/motivators**.

Example: Rodney Halvorson's Top Two Drivers

Like Avi, Rodney Halvorson is a senior executive at the same Fortune 50 financial services firm. He and Avi have the same top two motivators, but you can see how they play out in his life a bit differently because his life experience is different than Avi's.

#1: Utilitarian

Rodney is all about getting a return on investment. He will invest his resources (his time, talent, money, etc.) as long as he can see a direct outcome. This is true for himself and for his family. He is integrating his family, his children, into his practice. He makes sure he models and influences all he does to pragmatically prepare his children for life. He also treats all of his clients as extended family. He is pragmatic with the use of his playtime by exclusively participating in social activities that allow him to integrate family and clients, who are viewed as extensions of his family.

#2: Individualistic

This characteristic describes someone who is driven to have control over his own destiny and the destiny of others. Again, this motivator will drive this person to ascend: to be the captain of the squad, leader of the group, owner of a company, President of the United States — and in Rodney's case, to be an entrepreneurial, independent provider for his family, to control/positively affect the destiny of his family by inviting his children into his practice, and leading with legacy in mind, for his family and his clients.

Rodney's Unique Attributes feedback included the following:

- Highest level of integrity
- Exemplary father
- Dedicated to clients
- Relentless client service
- Treats teammates like family
- Participative leader
- Smart
- Focused
- Structured
- Self-made
- Guides others
- Community driven — teacher/coach
- Organized

- High standards
- Personally invested
- Honorable
- Interested / interesting
- Unemotional
- Genuine
- Sports fan
- Well put-together

His unique message reflects his top two motivators, how he views himself via his Introspection journey, and how he authentically shows up in life as is reflected by his Unique Attributes feedback:

"As a financial advisor I bring a holistic approach to financial planning. I help my clients across their banking, wealth structuring and credit needs.

"Anyone who knows me knows I am a family man. I have integrated my kids into my business and my clients are truly extended family. We all socialize together as well as work together — clients, kids, all of us. I live a transparent life where integrity is paramount. It's not something I speak about, but it's something I model everyday for my clients and my kids."

It is clear to see that while these two people have similar roles in the same firm and share the same two key drivers that motivate them personally, they are distinctly and uniquely different individuals. And, they need to attract two distinct audiences.

In this way Avi and Rodney get to be who they are, connected to their purpose, energized by what they do. This is aligning your purpose, passion and profit!

> When you take the time to explore what your unique differences are and learn how to effectively communicate them, you will create a sustainable demand for your brand.

Communicate to Connect

I worked with an institution where the research department was to inform the Senior Executive Leadership team regarding Analytics to help drive strategy.

As is often the case, a key issue in this dynamic is translating from tech talk to what I call Customer Point of View. If the researchers cannot adequately relay their great work, adoption by the Senior Executives doesn't reach its full potential, and tension potentially exists between the groups because of mutual frustration.

While intellectually understanding the business objective, the researchers still may not be effective at making the translation. They are about white papers versus story, logic versus emotion, data points versus connecting the dots. Now, this could be an entirely effective, in fact, appropriate communication strategy — if they were advising scientists. However, in this instance they are advising executives of a high-end services business. The disconnect is palpable, and we are working to help the researchers recognize and understand their audience's point of view.

There is a distinction between *communicating* and *communicating to connect*. Communicating to connect asks, "How do you share what makes you different in a way that attracts others?"

Each of us communicates all day with people: at home with our spouse, at work with our colleagues, at the store with clerks, at the gym with trainers, on the phone, etc. Or at least we think we do. We talk, and we may listen — but do we necessarily connect? Do we feel heard? Do we understand someone else? Did they understand us? Buy into us? Our idea? Our project? Our point of view?

Did you play the "telephone game" when you were a kid, where you make a circle and the first person whispers a message to the next, and so on? The message gets relayed around the circle and then the last person, usually with total bewilderment, says some crazy thing that makes little to no sense, and the entire room cracks up! Of course the message never made it around the circle as it started: someone misunderstood something, didn't hear something, and the next thing you know you can see the "disconnect" that has occurred.

This is a great metaphor for what happens all day, every day. I've been consulting on effective communication for over 20 years with literally tens of thousands of people, and I can tell you definitively that when it comes to communication, very simply, one size does not fit all.

In all these years, I have never had anyone say to me, "Really, Michele? I think I can communicate the same with everyone and it always works well." And I don't believe it's because they are being polite. We all know intellectually and experientially that everyone is not the same, and we cannot expect to effectively communicate with everyone the same way.

And yet, "disconnects" (as I call them) occur all day, every day. On one end it may just be a simple misunderstanding. I didn't understand you or you didn't understand me; no big deal. On the other end it may be all-out conflict: "I just cannot work with that person," for example. In between the two ends, there are myriad areas of disconnect. For example, someone gets their feelings hurt because they were left out of the communication loop on something, or because of the way someone spoke to them — or didn't speak to them. Or someone feels disrespected because they were not invited to participate in a meeting, or be on a project — or lead the project. And, of course, you can fill in the blanks with all of the other disconnects based on your own observations in your daily experiences.

I have concluded long ago that one of two things is occurring. Either (1) we don't know how to communicate differently, or (2) for any number of reasons, we know how to communicate differently but we just aren't choosing to do so.

Customer Point of View

Sometimes people believe they are just too busy to bother adjusting their communication, or the circumstance doesn't warrant the effort to ensure they are communicating to connect.

I find that when people tell me they are too busy and they just don't have time to call or email to explain something or better understand something, the truth is that they didn't create the time to spend thinking in advance about the person they are meeting with and how they would best relate. Or perhaps they just didn't want to slow down and take the time to explain exactly how they wanted something done, or they felt that the other person should have known what to do without explanation. But the time they don't have up front they will end up allocating on the back end to clean something up. I advocate you spend the time preparing up front rather than cleaning up messes on the back end!

So often we give much effort and attention to doing something well and then fall short when it comes time to execute, implement or engage. And all that good work done with pride and possibly passion ends in disappointment and even disgust. But who is in control here? Great news... you!

Imagine that you have spent a good amount of time thinking about hosting a special event. You've researched the menu, purchased everything, made favorite foods for each of the guests, even made foods that were based on a few who have dietary restrictions — vegan, low sugar, gluten free. But all you said when you invited everyone was, "We would love to have you come for dinner." You didn't tell them what the menu was, or that you were making favorite foods, or you didn't communicate to the individuals with special diets that you were preparing foods just for them. Do you think some people might not accept your invitation? Would you be more likely to encounter last-minute cancellations? The guests are just not as invested as if you had shared what very likely would have mattered most to them, from their perspective.

Let's get in front of this train instead of being dragged along behind it. To do so, you need to first understand what your audience cares about, and then learn how to communicate how you are addressing their "care-about" in a way that is designed to make sure you connect with them from their point of view.

It's essential to look at how differently people receive information and what they are wired to care about. We don't all receive information the same way, and we are not all inspired by the same things. And even when we do care about the same things, it's for our own unique reasons.

If you don't understand this, then all your work on aligning your Purpose with your Passion from the Inside Out may not resonate with your audiences, and this would not allow you to tie up your Purpose and Passion with your Profit. And that just wouldn't be acceptable -- not to me. Otherwise I wouldn't be keeping my promise to you that this book will show you how to align your Purpose, Passion and Profit. And so we will!

Recognize, Understand, and Adapt to Connect

It is just as important to be aware of *how* we communicate as well as *what* we are communicating.

> Attracting our audience to our Unique Message can succeed or fail based on how we deliver it.

There are four areas of behavior it is *critical* to understand with regard to how we go about creating connection with others. None of these are better or worse; good or bad — they just are!

(This is another area where assessments are utilized to help clients understand themselves and the impact they are having on others. To learn about your behavioral style and recognize your impact, you can use the same tool as our coaching clients. For more information, go to **Skilset.com/styles**.)

#1: How we go about influencing others

Some of us do this using *emotion*. We build relationships, engage in conversation, tell stories, use humor, wit, charm, enthusiasm, etc., to persuade.

Others of us approach influencing others by using *logic*. We use data, facts, proof points, and straightforward dialogue. We are undemonstrative when looking to influence others.

If you aren't aware of this, and you operate with emotion to influence someone who connects through logic, for example, you will at best minimize the connection and at worst polarize the other person. You'd want to be mindful that no matter how excited or enthusiastic you are about something, you don't want to share that excitement by being loud or giddy or overly emotional if your intended audience is influenced by logic. You'd want to share your point of view by explaining the impact potential, how you arrived at it, and why it's valuable. In other words, don't communicate in Spanish if the other person communicates in French!

#2: How we pace ourselves

Some of us are just wired to be *fast*. We think fast, talk fast, and make decisions quickly. We think about the big picture, and/or we focus in on the bottom line and the results.

Some of us are wired to be *slow*. We need time to digest the information, to think about it, to reach conclusions. We are considering the process for adopting or implementing, and/or we may be researching and further analyzing information to verify and validate, thus needing more time.

If we are unaware of these differences, we may speak so quickly or in a rambling (non-linear) style so that the other person didn't actually have time to process what we were saying. As a result, they may not connect with us — *even if they might have agreed with our point of view!*

When we are comfortable expressing ourselves and we are fast paced, we may think that silence from others equals agreement, when in reality they may not agree at all — they're just not comfortable sharing their thoughts out loud, or they're not ready to respond because they may need more time to know what they think. "Checking in" with people who aren't speaking up after a meeting is a good idea, and it needs to occur in an environment that is "safe" — i.e., one-on-one, not in a group.

#3: How we respond to rules and regulations

Some of us *want to know the rules* so we can follow them and operate within those parameters. We want things done accurately and systematically.

Others are *self-willed and independent* by nature: they would prefer not to be constrained by rules.

Those who follow the rules will be well informed and may want to inform others accordingly, whereas those who are more free-wheeling may not need or even want the details but rather just want to move things forward if there are no major obstacles to be addressed.

#4: How we problem solve

Essentially we can categorize problem solving into three variable approaches:

a. Yeah! Bring it on! I'll take the risk, take the hit and take it on.
b. Avoidance! Hope it dissipates, wait and see if it just takes care of itself.

c. Consensus building: applying a team approach, not seeing things as win and lose but cooperation and compromise.

People with different approaches to problem solving may all be interested in you, your services, your product, or your offer, but they may be turned off by your approach to them if you are unaware of their individual strategies.

The bottom line is this:

> When it comes to communication, one size does <u>not</u> fit all!

What does that mean exactly? Well, it means that we cannot communicate the same way with everyone — in the way that is most natural to us, to our style — and expect that it will necessarily resonate with everyone else. We may just be wired differently. Think about creating a document on a PC and sending it over to a Mac, or vice versa: punctuation drops out, bullets become letters, etc. PCs and Macs have different operating systems; they process the same information differently. So it is with people. We too are wired differently.

To communicate effectively, we must first recognize how we are wired — how we operate. Next, we need to recognize how the "others" (those that are not our same style) are wired. Then, we must move beyond recognition or awareness to understanding — really coming to understand *how* we are different, what that looks like, and why that is so. When we understand this, we can then realize that people are not "doing something to us," intentionally being difficult, seemingly out to get us, waking up in the morning with the intention of making us crazy, frustrating us, etc. They are simply being who they are.

Once we realize how we are different from others, we could move into tolerating one another. But if we truly *understand* the differences, we can skip over toleration and move straight ahead into appreciation. Our differences actually allow us to see things more broadly. Differences help us to notice important details and pay attention to concerns that might improve our product, our service, the client experience, or our relationship with someone.

> What I'm describing we call Beach Ball Communication.

Imagine this exercise: You are standing with your nose touching one of those multicolored inflatable beach balls. From where you stand, you see an orange, white, and yellow panel. Someone else — a colleague, a client, a boss, an employee, a teacher, a parent, a teenager — is standing on the other side with their nose against the very same beach ball. But they see a red, white, and green panel.

How can this be? You are both looking at the very same object: a beach ball. How can you be seeing such different things?

How would you solve this mystery? You would have to walk around to see what they are seeing; what they are looking at. And they would have to do the same.

When you are willing to stop and consider looking at something to understand how someone else is seeing it, then you have the opportunity to recognize how they see it differently, to actually understand how that is so, and then to appreciate what they see.

Most often, however, people only stay on their side of the beach ball. They only see things from their perspective, and they end up defending their position, perhaps even arguing over it. They're often frustrated because the other person is disputing what they *know* to be true.

Here's the lesson: As my client, Gaye, expressed it, "You have to begin by meeting someone where they are — on the other side of the beach ball — before you can bring them over to your point of view."

This is what is needed when you create your Unique Value Proposition, or Your Unique Selling Proposition. You must look at what you think is valuable about you from your *audience's* point of view. What do they care about? Then you can consider what you deem valuable and make sure it aligns with what is meaningful from your target audience's perspective.

A coaching client of mine recently shared with me how early on he had influenced his family to allow him to come to the United States from India to study. The family valued independence and high-level education. They wanted their son to be able to support himself, live well, have choices and, most importantly, get an excellent education.

He, on the other hand, wanted to go to work. So he worked hard and graduated high school two years early. He then found an accelerated advanced degree program that would allow him to graduate from college two years earlier than normal, and he found it in the U.S. at a highly prestigious institution. He had the grades to get in and was accepted. Next, he researched an employer who would put him through an expedited executive leadership program while he was in their employ.

The family didn't want him to go to the U.S., but he had found a way to graduate early from high school, a top-notch school to get into and graduate early again, and then an employer who would support taking his education to another level. He fulfilled all of his parents' criteria. He aligned what he wanted and what he valued with *their* core "care-abouts." As a result, he got to do what he wanted, which was to get a job and start building his career.

This is an example of meeting your audience (in this case, his parents) where they are, before he could take them where he wanted to go — getting started on his career in the U.S. No surprise, today he is a senior executive in a Fortune 1000 company.

When we find ourselves feeling frustrated by someone who isn't seeing what we are trying to share, or when we are not seeing what the other person cares about, it is a reminder that "beach ball communication" is a choice we can exercise. Just mentally pull out a beach ball and visualize walking around to the other side to see what they see. You may be surprised.

A positive by-product of seeing from the other person's viewpoint is that when they experience you being open to considering their perspective, they will likely be far more receptive to yours. And once you have each looked at things more broadly than you would have independent of each other, you may reach new heights. You will very likely develop an appreciation for one another and a mutual respect moving forward.

In truth, you're in control of managing your frustrations with another person. They don't have a "beach ball" — but NOW you do! Give it a try. You will forever change the trajectory of your interactions. You won't just be "communicating": you will be able to communicate to connect!

As we now understand, communicating to connect is not a one-size fits all proposition. Can you think of people who you would characterize as:

- Forceful, direct, and results-oriented?
- Optimistic, engaging and talkative?
- Steady, patient and relaxed?
- Precise, well-informed and detail oriented?

As we think of each of these different styles of people it becomes clear *why* one size just cannot fit all. These people have very different needs and very different words that will attract them. Below are practical clues on how to deliver your unique message so it is well received.

Know what your audience responds/reacts to:		
4 Unique Core Needs	**Words That Will Connect**	**Words That Will Cause Disconnect**
Results	Bottom line Faster Forward	Patient Follow directions Delayed
Engagement	Interaction People Fun	Standard Structured Quietly
Security	Consistent Help Safe	Urgent Confrontation Unexpected
Information	Data Thinking Formula	Experimental Educated guess Assumption

So, how does this work when you are communicating with a diverse group of people — when doing public speaking, or conducting a meeting, for instance? Here's a sample statement incorporating a mix of the key words to ensure you connect across a broad audience, so that each person will feel as though you have connected with them.

"I look <u>forward</u> to sharing some <u>thinking</u> with you today to <u>help</u> you learn how to <u>interact</u> with <u>people</u> in the ways that will create <u>fast</u> and <u>consistent</u> results."

So far, we've covered a lot of brand territory. Now that you understand...

- Who you are (Step One: Introspection)
- What makes you unique (Step Two: Differentiation)
- How to message to your customer point of view (Step Three: Unique Message)

You're ready to take a look at the best-fit way for you to congruently get your message out (Step Four: Creating Brand Buzz).

The great news is… knowing your purpose, from Part One – Discovery, will definitely help guide you!

And in the next chapter you'll get to see how others (Ivan and Dianne) have specifically aligned their choices for creating Brand Buzz with their purpose.

6

Step Four: Creating Brand Buzz — Let Your Purpose Guide You

"Without promotion something terrible happens... nothing."

— PT BARNUM

L ET'S BEGIN STEP FOUR by getting this out on the table first: *There is no one right way to create buzz around your brand.* In fact, the "right way" should simply be the most congruent fashion that is aligned with your purpose. Nothing that feels awkward or unnatural for you is going to be the right way to create brand buzz.

That being said, let's get this out also: many of us have belief systems that we need to re-check. For example, I have worked with hundreds of people with this particular concern: "I was brought up to think it was not appropriate to brag about oneself."

Are you afflicted with this "dis-ease" about speaking about yourself? Many of those hundreds (amongst the thousands I have worked with) were brought up in the Midwest of the U.S., or in Japan and other regions of the world where this mindset is part of the culture. So I developed a scale to help people understand the impact of that thinking.

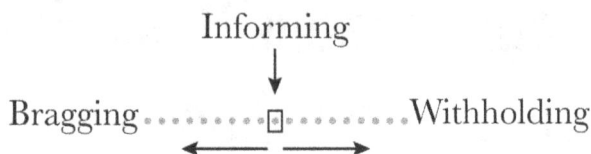

Informing
↓
Bragging ....□.......... Withholding
←—— ——→

On the opposite end of the Bragging scale is Withholding. In the center is Sharing or Informing. I think most people feel quite comfortable informing, particularly when it is focused on how to be of help to someone else.

I'm going to assume, having come through Steps One through Three, that you recognize you are a miracle, here for a purpose and you have value. If this is true, then it is essential that you realize that *not* sharing with others the value that you bring is completely out of alignment with living your purpose.

So, with love in my heart, I will say to you, *get over it!*

Focus on who you are trying to be of value to, and look at you from their point of view. What will they want and need to know? And where are they most likely to be looking for you? This will help give you ease when it comes to sharing about yourself or your offering, and informing others so they can recognize your value to them.

There are many vehicles you can access to help get the word out about you. You want to let your purpose be your guide. Ideally, you have allowed your purpose to be your driver for Steps One and Two — Introspection and Differentiation, as well as Your Unique Message, Step Three — and it will be so now in Step Four. Let purpose guide you to your best marketing choices for you to create brand buzz. (It can, and should, continue to be your guidepost in Step Five, Maintenance, directing your ongoing choices as well.)

For me, I am very clear that I am here to inspire others to reach their full potential by aligning their purpose, passion and profit. It's such a miracle that you are even here — how can you not honor that by being your best self? And how could it be appropriate to hide that away from others because of some discomfort you were raised to believe, or some notion that you have nothing of value to contribute? Pretty silly, wouldn't you agree?

My best way to exhibit my passion and live in my purpose is to actively inspire others. And I can give the most value through opportunities where I can be engaged with others in an interactive way. (Remember, one of my key drivers is Utilitarian, which translates into, I truly want people to get the most value and usefulness from any engagement with me. Thus, even in a book format I am providing you several takeaway tools.)

Early in my career I recognized that I had to overcome my fear of public speaking or I wouldn't be able to be my best at helping people get the greatest value from what I had to offer. Over 20 years ago, I mentioned to one of my amazing mentors, Dr. Tessa Warschaw, that I thought I should start looking at doing some public speaking engagements. She was listening, and within a month I got a call from an event planner inviting me to participate in my first professional (i.e., paid) speaking engagement. Dr. Tess told me what they were looking for, what to charge, and how to negotiate the contract. The next thing I knew I was in Spokane, Washington, alongside her at a medical retreat. There were 800 — yes, *eight hundred* — people in the audience at my first speaking engagement! I learned a lot. The event planner and the audience were satisfied. And I got even better. (If you meet me in person or at one of my workshops, ask me on a break to share the story of HOW I got better. It involves a video camera in my bedroom and a police squad.)

Sometimes I still get just a little queasy right before I go on stage, or into a workshop, or an on-air interview. When that happens, I recognize immediately that I am focused in the wrong direction: I'm thinking about me, not my audience, in that moment, and why I'm there, which is to serve. They aren't concerned with what I look like or any number of self-focused things my mind might have jumped to. All they care about is learning something they can use immediately that makes a positive impact in their lives. As soon as I get back to that, I'm comfortable, and I can't wait to make that happen for them.

Let's focus in on the four top ways you might want to consider creating your brand buzz: *networking, speaking, writing,* and *leveraging social media.* I'll share some interesting and creative ways my graduates align their purpose with their promotion, and I will share some resources that may prove helpful for you along the way.

Four Ways to Create Brand Buzz
Strategy, Tools, and Tips

SPEAKING	WRITING
Presentations	Book
Keynotes	Blog
Workshops	Articles

STEP FOUR: Brand Buzz

NETWORKING	SOCIAL MEDIA
Attending	Relevance
Associations / Committees	VLOG
Events	FB Live
Organizations	Distribution Channels

#1: Networking

Whether it is standing up and introducing yourself at the beginning of an industry meeting, being introduced at a board meeting, or e-networking on LinkedIn, networking is the most typical way in which people will create brand buzz.

The key to networking is to remember that you are not there to sell. Instead, you are there to meet people and learn how you can provide value to them/be of service to them.

Are you a person who finds networking to be uncomfortable or awkward? Most people do. It's a manufactured environment and it feels a bit unnatural. Speaker, author and networking expert Omar Periu offers a list of what he identifies as the 7 Best Networking Questions for you to ask. Perhaps you can draw upon them on your next networking outing:

1. How did you get your start in this business?
2. What do you enjoy most about what you do?
3. What separates your company from your competition?
4. What advice would you give someone just getting started in your business?
5. What do you see as the coming trends in your business?
6. What ways have you found to be most effective for promoting your business?
7. What one sentence would you like people to use in describing the way you do business?

I'm partial to #1 because it reflects taking a sincere interest in the individual; what's their history, their story? I also find #5 sets up conversation about possibility and the future. That allows you to enter into this person's future potentially. And #7 helps you to gain clarity of understanding as to what they do and how they do it. Knowing this will guide how you can be of real value to them.

Networking is an investment in your most precious resource: your time. You want to be both sincere with those you meet while being strategic with how much time you are spending with that person.

Here's a networking secret that may at first blush appear reversed, but it is not: if you do not think the person you have met is someone you want to re-engage with (because they aren't your target audience or are not connected to that audience), then you want to be prepared to provide value for them on the spot. Go ahead and share your top-level resources, or direct and guide them to a source — a book, an organization — and leave it at that.

However, if you think this is someone you *would* like to re-engage with, do *not* share with them in that environment. Rather, tell them about the resources you would like to share with them — connections, contacts, information — and then say that you will need to locate that information to send to them later, or you will broker an introduction over coffee or lunch for them, etc. Then offer to contact them again in the next 24 hours with the resources you have promised. This sets up a future connection that could turn into a profitable relationship for you both.

Always be prepared to follow up.

Networking doesn't end when you leave the event: it ends after you go home and take care of any follow-up (even if only sending a note to say "I will follow up with you when I return to my office next week"). Otherwise, send back the information you promised, get the calendar lined up for a next meeting, request LinkedIn Connections while people remember you, and so on. Take the time to make your follow-up message personal.

Mention something you heard them say or you observed — something that will show them that you are genuinely interested in them.

Don't forget to think in terms of how to best communicate with each person as well. You may want to go back to Step Three and re-visit Communicate to Connect to determine the different needs and language you want to use. Using that model, following up from a networking event might look something like this:

"Hi (name), I was so glad to <u>learn </u>what you are working on and how it is <u>helping</u> (a person, solve a problem, etc.). I told you I had a <u>person</u> I wanted to introduce you to, as I am sure they are looking to get the same kind of <u>results</u>. I am sending an e-intro out to both of you momentarily as promised."

Creative Networking on a Whole Other Level

A. Unassuming third party endorsements

You should have certain tools at the ready to send following a networking event. For example, a colleague of mine, Robert Chesney, has a wonderful business where he creates video testimonials. There's nothing more impressive (or unassuming) than to have your clients, customers, audience speak on your behalf. He suggests that once you have your testimonials built out, you simply add a video link into the signature block of your email. That way, the testimonials are readily available without being conspicuous or having to tell people to go to your website to see something. (You don't want to make them work for it: always make it easy for someone to connect with you! This also includes always putting your contact info in your email signature block, by the way.)

B. Events

Some people attend events; some people, like Dianne, just create them to bring the right audience to her. Dianne is one of my IndiBrand™ grads, so I am able to show you how choosing events as the primary vehicle to create her Brand Buzz is in full alignment with Dianne's Purpose.

Background:

I first met Dianne over 20 years ago when we were both participating in a Quantum Leap workshop series developed by Dr. Tessa Warschaw. Dianne and I are both entrepreneurs with similar interests in self-development. Later, when I developed the IndiBrand program, she saw me, my work, my passion, and wanted in! (The right people find us when we are living in our purpose. I carefully select where I spend my learning and networking time, making sure these activities align with my purpose. I might be attracted to many other possibilities, but I let my commitment, to be aligned with my purpose, help me make prudent choices.)

Dianne's style:

She is an engagement-focused people person. Strangers are just friends she hasn't met yet.

Dianne's motivators:

She is Utilitarian. She will invest time/money, as long as there is a return on investment (ROI). She is practical and pragmatic. Her second driver is Individualistic. She wants to be in control of her own destiny and that of others — in a leading position with power to make things happen.

Dianne's purpose:

Connecting to create bigger outcomes for all.

Dianne's business:

Investment Banking and Executive Placement.

Dianne's strategy:

She is the founder of Amplify Roundtables, creating networking events that bring the right people for her together in a room. She finds a corporate host sponsor, one that is highly regarded in that industry and with just the right cache for physical ambience. Along with her email database, she personally pre-invites key attendees. Inviting them to her event gives her a reason to make contact with someone she's trying to meet. She then greets attendees and acts as their networking concierge at the event, introducing the right-fit people to one another, making sure they receive value from attending her events. Finally, she brings in a relevant speaker and she serves as Emcee.

Not only does she effortlessly pull together these events as a way to grow her business and connect her clients to one another, creating community, but she quite literally wrote the book on networking. Dianne is the author of PowerLadder: Network Your Way to Career Success.

C. Organizations

When it comes to organizations, there are two roads people usually travel. The first is to attend organization events as a guest. The second is to become a member of that community. The first, attending, has already been covered in the networking section. In the second scenario, becoming part of the community, here are a few special tips to maximize your impact:

Tip 1: Commit for a minimum of one year and contribute all out. Be of as much value as you can. People notice and will gladly introduce and refer you — and be your brand ambassador (that is, touting your value).

Tip 2: Join a committee. The best committee to join is the Membership committee. You will meet anyone joining the group and get to make a first impression with them directly.

Tip 3: A more targeted strategic approach may also be tied in with your purpose and your preferred method for creating brand buzz. For example, if you are a good writer and that is your chosen focus for creating brand buzz, you can offer to assist with event invites or the monthly/quarterly newsletter. It will also allow you to connect with key people in the organization and possibly in your industry for interviewing.

Tip 4: Or if your preferred method for creating brand buzz is speaking, you might want to join the Speaker Committee. This allows you to identify relevant speakers, interview them, and then connect with them at your event. You could see about partnering to help each other to book speaking engagements where the other is speaking.

Tip 5: If social media is your focus, be sure to use Facebook Live at the event to promote the organization. Post group shots on Instagram; or, with the speakers' permission, post a two- to five-minute segment of their talk on the organization's You Tube channel. You can post all of this on your accounts as well as the organization's.

If creating brand buzz via organizations excites you, you might consider creating your own organization — like my client, Ivan Rosenberg, does.

Background:

When I first met Ivan some 15 years ago, he was an entrepreneur looking to build out his brand. He had received his BS in Electrical Engineering and MS in Computer Science from Cornell University, and his PhD in Business and Management from the University of Rochester. Ego aside and always eager to learn, in his mid-50s Ivan signed up for my IndiBrand workshop. His story illustrates how when we are living our purpose, understanding our Differentiator, consciously identifying our Unique Messaging and actively engaged in creating Brand Buzz, the right people — YOUR right audience — will be magnetized to you. The magnetizing effect is true in business and true in every area of your life — as you will see with Ivan's story.

Ivan's style:

Ivan's style is an analytical, with a love of systems and process; he is a relationship person with a close-knit set of friends and family. He adapts to allow for more group interaction.

Ivan's motivators:

Ivan is Individualistic. He wants to be in control of his own destiny and that of others — in a leading position with power to make things happen. He also is Theoretical. He has a love of learning. He has the ability to become an expert in his chosen areas of interest.

Ivan's purpose:

Ivan wants to make a difference in the world by helping people / companies shift their perspectives and create breakthroughs that allow them to accomplish previously "impossible" goals by moving them into possibility where they saw none prior.

Ivan's business:

Productivity Breakthrough Consulting Practice.

Ivan's strategy:

He is the founder of InVista Associates. Initially Ivan created a healthcare networking group, but he realized this wasn't a financially prudent market for his practice and he wasn't as passionate about healthcare as he was about space. (Interestingly, space allows for world impact, which ties to his purpose).

Ivan had done work with Jet Propulsion Laboratory (JPL), Amgen and the W.M. Keck Observatory in Hawaii. I helped him to identify how to tailor a presentation he was giving at Goddard Space Flight Center to make sure he communicated to connect. He credits this with his getting that piece of business. He had also acted as professional coach to a world-renown astronaut. And now he was ready to go to new heights (bad pun intended).

In 2011 Ivan launched The Aerospace and Defense Forum. He started it in Los Angeles and now has seven forums across the country, including five in California, one in Texas and one in Arizona. He is planning expansion into other areas soon. These Forums allow him access to leaders in the Aerospace and Defense industry, his target audience. He is recognized as a significant influence in this market, helping missions get produced on time and on budget by creating "breakthrough" training for engineers and the project managers who lead these projects.

Ivan's purpose isn't only being fulfilled in his business practice: it applies to his life at large. Creating organizations to solve worldwide issues is part of Ivan's purpose. Ivan has two children, both of whom are autistic. He is passionate about eradicating the disempowering language of "disability" and replacing it with "unique ability." Both Sarah and Daniel are of college age now, and Ivan saw a unique talent in his children and across the autistic spectrum. These kids have the ability to work with incredible focus on repetitive tasks, which is a perfect fit for manufacturing.

So Ivan launched the organization, The Uniquely Abled Project. He assembled the board and created a partnership with a local community college, government agencies, and businesses to help young adults on the autistic spectrum be self-sufficient and uniquely contributing individuals in the work-force by playing to their particular strengths.

As part of this program they created The Uniquely Abled Academy, Matching Unique Skills to the Unique Needs of Manufacturers: Training Individuals to become CNC (Computer Numerical Control) Machine Operators. Not only are the typical characteristics of someone on the autistic spectrum a perfect match for a CNC operator, but there is also a huge unfulfilled demand for such operators across the country. The fit is so good that one employer reported that in less than two months the new hire (who eight months before didn't know what a CNC machine was) was among the best operators he had ever had.

To date The Uniquely Abled Academy has run its first full academic program and placed 11 out of the 11 students who participated in this first consort in gainful employment. The businesses are thrilled with their new hires and are seeing additional uniquely appropriate roles for these uniquely abled employees. A second class of 16 is currently under-way.

Ivan is a man who lives his purpose daily with passion and profit! As part of honoring and living in alignment with his life's purpose he creates organizations that allow others to be able to live theirs as well.

#2: Speaking

Being a speaker is another key way to build buzz around your brand. Everyone knows the statistic that the fear of public speaking (also known as *glossophobia*) is the number one fear, affecting 74% of the public — 75% of women and 73% of men.

In surveys, it even outweighs fear of spiders and death! It's pretty clear that we all need to overcome it in one way or another.

While not everyone is interested in being a keynote speaker or something as grand as, say, giving a TED talk, most executives need to speak in front of their teams, and maybe also at large industry conferences. Salespeople need to present to buying teams; and everyone needs to "sell their ideas" (see Daniel Pink's book, *To Sell Is Human*) and gain "buy-in" from time to time.

Most people realize that improving their ability, if not their comfort level, to speak publicly will have impact on their career trajectory. Ideally the goal is to work on their ability to present in an inspiring, persuading or informative way that is appropriate to their particular situation, and to create engagement, understanding and connection with their audience(s).

What most of us *don't* realize is that people with certain styles (as you saw in Step One, Communicating to Connect) find pubic speaking uncomfortable not only in front of large groups but also in a team meeting. They may have trouble even speaking one-on-one unless they feel a sense of trust and safety with the other person. Then there are others whose style is to absolutely speak up in every circumstance. They want to be heard, seen, express themselves — and they will step up, step out, take the risk, take the hit, and move toward the goal line.

I was coaching a client yesterday who is working on building up his speaking skill set. Because I always want to know what the evaluation metrics will be to determine progress and success in any client coaching relationship, I asked what he wanted as a speaker. Specifically, he said he wants to:

- Feel more comfortable internally

- Not rely on notes
- Not talk too fast (hurrying to get it over with)
- Make sure his points are coming across clearly

These are all quite normal and appropriate goals for anyone who needs to speak in public in any situation. This client's communication style makes him uncomfortable speaking up in any setting, so for him, the lessons learned will be just as applicable for one-on-one meetings, meetings with groups at the office, and publicly.

Here are a few key tips to help you develop as a speaker:

Tip 1: *Know your material.* Don't speak on a subject you are not intimately knowledgeable about.

Tip 2: *Be prepared.* Know your audience — what do they care about? You are presenting to them for their benefit.

Tip 3: *Practice.* Rehearse your presentation. Don't memorize it, but know the order and the flow; do memorize your transitions from one slide to the next or one sub-topic to the next. And time yourself — nothing is worse than not getting to complete. (Consider using the video on your phone or computer so you can playback how you appear, looking for congruent hand movements or any distracting gestures, and how you sound.)

Tip 4: *Flip the order.* Start with the key takeaway first. Most people build up to it. But you may run out of time, or you may have a key person in your audience who needs to leave early. You want to grab their attention right at the start, then you can go back and fill in the details, provide stats if that's relevant, tell stories to help them engage, re-call, re-tell, and conclude in a way that reinforces where you started.

While this section is not intended to be a "speaker presentation" training, there are a couple of items that come up so frequently I feel compelled to share them with you here. They are priceless to both your comfort level and your success when speaking.

Bonus Tip #1: I've been consulting with Fortune 500 companies for two decades. Most of the companies, executives and salespeople I work with (and/or their departments assembling the presentations) start their speeches by establishing their own credibility. "Been in business since 2006... 500 clients... exceeded projections year over year..." etc. But the truth is, you haven't even earned their interest yet. They want to know what you can do for them. THEN if they are still interested, they will want you to back it up and provide your credibility. Subconsciously the real reason people start their presentation here is to give themselves confidence; to hopefully prove themselves worthy of listening to. In truth, that credibility slide should be the second to last slide of the presentation.

Bonus Tip #2: Be bold = be comfortable. While this seems like an oxymoron if you are nervous to be bold, it simply means, focus on THEM, not YOU. When your attention is on yourself, your thoughts may look like:

- *I hope I sound smart (or I hope I don't sound stupid).*
- *I hope they don't ask me any questions I don't know how to answer.*
- *I don't want to forget what I'm saying.*
- *I wish I was 10 pounds lighter.*
- _____ [Fill in the blank.]

This line of thinking is what makes someone nervous. That's why I advocate that speaking is the one time you shouldn't go inside. Instead, you should focus externally (after you've studied your material and practiced, of course). When you focus on your audience rather than yourself, your thinking sounds like this:

- *I want them to know how XYZ will help them.*
- *I know my stuff. And I can either answer their question on the spot or I'm confident committing to investigating and circling back.*
- *I have a deck or reference notes as placeholder that I can look at to remind me where I was if I digress.*
- *When I have fun, they have fun. If I am focused on myself and get nervous, I'll make them uncomfortable. I choose to make this about them, not me.*
- *They aren't interested in what I look like; they're interested in what I can do for them.*

Bonus Tip #3: For those of you aspiring to do a TED Talk you can get some additional tips created after my first year of Speaker Coaching for TEDx at **Skilset.com/TEDtips**.

Beyond Corporate Speaking

Many people successfully use speaking as a way to create exposure to new and prospective clients. It acts as a lead-generation step in new business development. Speaking can be done for free and it can also be done for fee.

This could look like my former-employee-turned-entrepreneur, Mishele Vieira, speaking at a Chamber of Commerce meeting. She has a business, Away with Chaos, designed to help people de-clutter so they can make room for what is most important in their lives. She helps people understand the barriers they may not recognize are keeping them held hostage to their "stuff," mess, or clutter, and she helps people with up-coming move/re-location strategies. Invaluable! (Perhaps you're familiar with the fact that moving only follows death and divorce on the list of life's stresses.)

I myself speak at conferences, company events, and host independent retreats. This is my favorite vehicle for engagement. I speak on several subjects, depending on the needs of the audience. Of course, *Create Demand For Your Brand* is a signature talk, as are *Communicate to Connect, DISCovering the Value of Your Team* and *The Power of CHOICE: Consistently, Honing, Our, Intentions, Concerning, Excellence*™. However, I actually prefer workshops to keynotes. I find workshops to allow a deeper level of engagement and interaction. I am able to inspire transformation in that environment, whereas keynotes typically allow for motivation or information.

If you are wondering what characterizes keynotes and workshops, and how they differ, here is a short overview.

A keynote speech refers to a relatively short speech, running from between 30 to 90 minutes. It is a one-way interaction: the speaker speaks and the audience listens. It often has an element of entertainment associated with it. It might involve a story, video, props or another type of visual. Keynote speakers are often seen as showmen (and women). They are more motivational than transformational. A keynote is also delivered, meaning the speaker talks and the audience listens with little or no interaction.

A workshop is usually anywhere from two to six hours or more in length. It absolutely allows for interaction. The "audience" is more participatory. A workshop often incorporates facilitated group or audience "partnershipping" exercises and verbal exchanges between the presenter and the audience. There's an opportunity for self-discovery and pragmatic application. Some movement around the room by participants is plausible in a workshop.

Speaking as Your Brand

For some people speaking is a way of life. It's what they do; it's how they make a living. Often they are also authors. If you are familiar with Wayne Dyer and/or Hay House Publications, this is a prime example of speaking as the brand, not just creating brand buzz.

Another example of speaking as being the brand has been underway for a very long time. You can trace this profession back and an example of how it has existed with the development of the National Speakers Association (NSA) back in 1973. NSA is a collective of more than 3,400 members, who include experts in a variety of industries and disciplines. NSA members reach audiences as speakers, trainers, educators, humorists, motivators, consultants, authors and more.

Today, with the accessibility of social media outlets and learning itself taking alternative formats, in combination with the rapid changes in career paths and professions largely due to technology, there is a movement whereby people are actively seeking their learning from forums like TED talks, salons, and speakers on stage, targeting specific information areas people want to learn about.

One of the queens of this movement would be Lisa Sasevich, who actually teaches how to sell from the stage in her signature *Speak to Sell* programs. She is known as the Queen of Sales Conversion and making the "irresistible offer." She's made a $30 million business out of it, and her firm has been on *INC's* Fastest Growing Private Companies list more than once. I've met with Lisa and also seen her in action, and she is a force, to be sure!

#3: Social Media

There is so much to be leveraged today through social media, with all the different outlets and tools and vehicles at our fingertips. And I've learned it takes a village. Know your audience! Create relevant content. Identify distribution channels.

If you're in any career you have to be on LinkedIn. It is the online source for networking. It gives you access to people, to jobs, to relevant communities. You can post on Facebook, Instagram, YouTube, and on and on. You can take a picture of yourself anywhere all day. But why?!

> The key word here is "relevance."

If it makes sense to create a VLOG (video blog), do it. If your business is showing how to do make-up application, it makes sense! If you're a physical therapist, you can show exercises. If you're a speaker, it's another "stage" of sorts.

Here's what I know: I'm not a techie! But I love connecting with people to inspire them to be their fullest version of themselves. If this means creating a studio in our office so we can turn on the camera and offer value to our membership community, I'm in. If it means recording bonus tips to expand upon content referenced in workshops, great! If it helps us launch this book and make it available to the largest number of "right-fit" people we can assist, I'm in! I'm looking forward to getting our testimonials converted from flat print to our clients speaking about the workshops and the book: real people connecting with real people!

I also know it takes a village. I actually resisted using social media for quite a long period because I thought I had to learn how to do it all myself. It's not my nature and it feels like it derails my focus from my purpose. I finally realized, like everything else, it's about assembling a great team!

It's the very essence of what I teach in my *DISCovering the Value of Your Team* workshop. Each of us has our own unique list of value we bring into an organization. (If you took the behavioral assessment mentioned earlier, you can find your unique value on page 4 of the report. Go to **Skilset.com/styles** to learn more.) Our task is to recognize them, understand them, skip over tolerating each other and truly learn to appreciate each other's value. And when we add my list to your list, and your list to another's, we create a broad and deep set of value that we can leverage. It will likely mean we need to learn to look past the behaviors that come as part of the package of our differences that could otherwise derail us. My frustration understanding tech jargon, for example, or my brilliant geeks being able to keep pace with my creativity and urgent sense of time could annoy us, frustrate us and derail us. But we have learned to truly appreciate those differences, because the value is so much greater collectively and allows us to achieve outrageous goals!

I have someone who worked at DirectTV helping us set up our studio right now. I have another helping us with an updated social media strategy. I have a video editor. I am always looking for the right resources and strengthening our team of talent so I can focus on what I do best: living in my purpose, creating content and engagement to influence and inspire.

#4: Writing

One area where I embraced on-line distribution channels early on was writing. People are looking for content all the time: contributors on blogs, online publications, e-books, or

PDFs that can go on your site or can be posted on other's sites, and so on. But if you are one of the thousands of people who think of writing as tough, or complicated, or just something that you're "not good at," I want to give you every assurance that you can write.

> Let's start, as is always my preference, from the inside out: If you can think it, you can write it!

This is not only true but it's also easier to support this statement today than it has ever been in our history. Why? Because editors abound. You can find editors on Craig's List — English teachers with MA's who will edit for incredibly reasonable rates. Or you can go to Upwork (formerly e-lance) or Fiverr and find editors. (Or you could work with my editor on this project, Vicki St. George of Just Write Editorial & Literary Services.) Or you can find a Virtual Assistant... and so on and so on and so on. The resources are plentiful. Accessing good copywriting talent or copy editors or even ghostwriters is no longer reserved only for big-time ad agencies or publishers. If you have a computer, or a smart phone for that matter, you have the ability to write because you can reach people who can help you out.

I recently read a note from Reid Tracy, president of Hay House, who writes a weekly newsletter. His inspiration I think is a good "thought starter" for writing. I also see it as a great way to get closer to your purpose. When you start to see what stands out to you in your week you'll recognize both what is and isn't important to you, what is and isn't meaningful, energizing, inspiring to you — all clues on the trail to discovering your purpose. However you may find it useful, here's what Reid Tracy had to share from his own process:

"... Try and write a weekly newsletter to yourself, or your Facebook friends, for the next four weeks. Here's how it works: You have to have your writing done each Sunday, no exceptions. It doesn't have to

be long or even well written. In other words, it's really about the mes-sage. Just pay attention to your day-to-day experiences and share what you experienced and what you learned. If you take this assign-ment, I bet you will be surprised by the things you notice in your week that you had been just glossing over in the past. And, if you are lucky, you will learn a little something about yourself, or someone may be helped by what you share!

I know what you might be thinking, why would anybody want to read what I have experienced? Let me share this. Every week as I write this newsletter I have doubts if anyone really cares or reads it. But when I see people at our Hay House events, I usually have hundreds of people come up to me and thank me for my newsletter! I try to re-member that as I look for inspiration in the prior week of my life.

Try it yourself and I'm sure you'll be surprised at how much you see, and how inspired you'll be."

You, Too, Can Write a Book

I don't recall the first time I was published, but I know that I've been writing, when inspired, for the past 25 years. I've written numerous workshops and corresponding workbooks. And I've written and delivered numerous talks. I have edited my own work in those instances, although I always had some-one in my office proofread as a second set of eyes for typos.

I have also written numerous articles and they have ap-peared in a wide array of business channels from Market-ingProfs.com (branding articles) to *The American Journal of Law* (networking, communication and new business development articles).

But the *pièce de résistance* has got to be the writing of this book. Have you ever wanted to write a book? Maybe you thought you weren't a good enough writer. Or you thought no one would want to read it if you did write it. Or you liked the idea but didn't know what you were interesting or well-versed enough in to author a book. Or you didn't know how. Or the most common thought perhaps... wait for it... you don't have enough time!

I wrote this list not based on research but based on my own self-talk for many, many years. The first few were fleeting thoughts but the last one — not enough time — that was the kicker! I own a company; we're in high demand = busy; I take care of parents; I... all very legitimate. UNTIL I came across Mike Koenigs.

If You Can Speak It, You Can Write It

Let me give full credit where credit is due. This is Mike's philosophy and the proof is in the publishing! Mike has "written" 10, yes, TEN, books. And he hasn't written a single word. That's because Mike is a speaker — both because he loves to talk and tell stories and excite and entice, but professionally he conducts seven-figure workshops and retreats as well.

Mike is the one who inspired me to finally create the first book. He has a program called Publish and Profit and he guides you on how to go about creating your #1 Bestselling Author book!

I can't say enough about Mike and his process. I do encourage any aspiring writer (or any existing author) to give Mike's program a look-see. A couple of key ideas involve his 10x10 process. Identify 10 key questions you are asked all the time about your business, work or passion (your topic area). Now identify 10 key questions your prospects, friends, community members (your target audience) *should* be asking. Next, get your smart phone out and start recording the answers. Send those recordings off for transcription (there are many sources available, I used Rev.com). Massage the transcripts or send them off to an editor saying, as only Mike could instruct, "Make this stuff into a book." I'm extrapolating one simple process I learned with Mike to show you how absolutely true it is that if you can speak you can write.

I did six 15-minute recordings and then I found myself preferring to actually write rather than record. It flowed more naturally for me through my hands, which was a little surprising to me being a speaker. The speaking and recording loosened me up and got me started and then I was on a writing roll.

Size Matters

I also want to share with you a bit of research I learned from Mike regarding the length of books and the likelihood of them being read through cover to cover. (Just in case you don't think you have enough material to fill an entire book, think again.)

Mike shared that the probability of someone reading your entire book actually *dwindles* with the corresponding length of your book. The likelihood someone will read your book cover to cover is:

- 30% for books up to 80 pages in length
- 20% for books between 120 and 200 pages
- 5% for books longer than 200 pages

Don't let the fear of not having enough material deter you from writing a book. And if you do have considerable material it may be a better strategy to break it up and write multiple shorter books than one longer one.

Additional Stats (and Excuse Busters)

You may be wondering if you have to have a book in print rather than an e-book. Here is another stat for you to consider. The chart below suggests readership was on a decline in 2015 for print books but on the rise for e-books. Perhaps you will want to consider self-publishing on Amazon Kindle and other e-book platforms like iBooks, Kobo, or Nook.

The Number of Book Readers Dips

% of adults who say they read at least one book in whole or in part in the previous 12 months

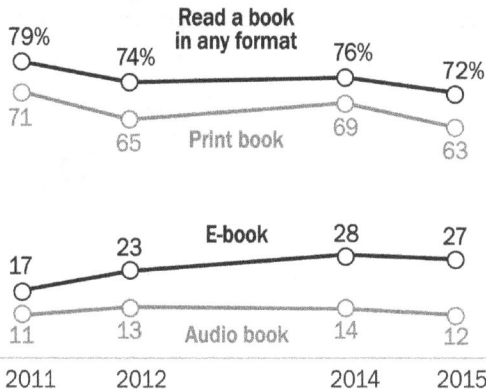

	2011	2012	2014	2015
Read a book in any format	79%	74%	76%	72%
Print book	71	65	69	63
E-book	17	23	28	27
Audio book	11	13	14	12

Source: Pew Research Center survey conducted March 17-April 12, 2015. N=1,907 adults.

PEW RESEARCH CENTER

Clarity Creates Possibility

As part of the Publish and Profit program I committed to completing the book in 90 days. It was one of the busiest periods in our company. I'm reminded of the adage, "Give something to a busy person if you want to get it done." Once you are in the groove, you just add one more thing into the mix and *voilà*, it gets done!

So how did I break through my biggest excuse for writing the book, lack of time?

The difference was for the first time, I saw the real possibility of how to actually write a book by simply speaking — and that was something I knew how to do! I had gained clarity, and clarity is what allows us to make choices we would not otherwise venture to make. You'll read more about this in the next chapter, Step Five: Maintenance — Aligning Your CHOICEs.

Are you ready? Let's get started with the final step in the five-step process. This is what keeps everything moving forward!

7

Step Five: Maintenance — Aligning Your CHOICEs

"Desire is the key to motivation, but it's determination and commitment to an unrelenting pursuit of your goal — a commitment to excellence — that will enable you to attain the success you seek."

— MARIO ANDRETTI

MAINTENANCE SOUNDS SO... WELL, BORING, even tedious, doesn't it? Where's the fun in that? Why "fun"? Because fun, however we might each interpret that, keeps us "fueled"!

In truth, this fifth step in building your brand by design, to create demand and live your life with purpose and passion while you profit, is actually the most exciting! This step embodies your life, day by day and choice by choice. What could be more exciting? We get to live our lives the way that we want, in ways that bring us true joy, that embody who we are, and allow us to be surrounded by those who appreciate us.

I understand you may still be struggling with the very real possibility of this way of being, even after all we've just walked through together in this book. So let me remind you of what you already now know...

> If you are choosing to recognize, understand and activate your purpose and create demand for your brand, you must start by knowing you are a miracle!

In order to live your life the way you want, with true joy, surrounded by those who appreciate you, you need to live your life conscious of the fact that you are a miracle... on a daily basis.

To some of you this may sound rather simple. To others, you may recognize this is not as easy as it sounds. In either case, you can look forward to discovering how you can do this as you read on.

Once I'm Done Building My Brand I'm Done, Right?

No. Maintenance, as I define Step Five, means having the awareness that everything, every day, is a choice. And those choices are either in or out of alignment with your purpose.

You'll be able to recognize this, assuming you've applied Steps One through Four already, by seeing that your choices are either taking you toward your dreams, goals and aspirations, or farther away.

Be reminded, this is about taking you closer toward YOUR dreams / goals / aspirations — not someone else's. (You may want to revisit Step One: Introspection, Authentic versus Synthetic Purpose.)

The choice then is to actively live your life on a daily basis consciously, re-embracing the fact you are a miracle and acknowledging your purpose (if you've already identified it) or acknowledging you are actively in search of it through your conscious state of self-reflection.

Let's break down what goes into making the choices that lead to aligning your purpose, passion and profit.

It was in my sincere effort to answer the ongoing inquiries around how I was creating such phenomenal success in my sales career that I first came up with the CHOICE model. The simple truth was that I realized, as I looked around the office in the sales organization of the company I was working for, that I was making different choices than my colleagues.

I was investing in myself. I was studying. I was attending targeted workshops and seminars. A longer story for another time as to why, but I was inspired to study self-awareness, communication and sales (in that order). I invested $60,000 of my then modest after-tax earnings over a three-year period. The company would give me the time off to go "do the work" on myself. They were smart. They watched my sales figures double, then triple each time I returned as I put just one new thing I had learned (or unlearned in some cases) into action. As a result, I ended up being amongst the top 2% of female earners in the nation before I was 30.

I knew my initial answer as to how I was creating my success — that "I was making different choices" — was too simplistic. While it was entirely true, that idea wasn't going to guide anyone who wanted to follow the same plan to create extraordinary results for themselves. (Worthy of noting: I later realized that contemplating the answer to this question was one of my markers, my key life experiences, and it provided another clue toward my own purpose, which is "guiding and inspiring others to achieve their full potential by aligning their purpose, passion and profit," as we discussed back in Step One: Introspection.)

It started with a desire — my desire was to make good on this sales opportunity I had been given. But, as happens, life veered me off course (or so I thought) with an early age divorce. I found it hard to concentrate on my work and my inability to focus was keeping me from doing a good job in my new role in sales. I was a pre-law major who graduated with honors from UCLA. I had worked five nights a week throughout my last three years of high school to buy a car and pay for the insurance and gas. I wasn't accustomed to failure. Struggle? Yes, sometimes; everything didn't come easily. But failure? No.

People start out with desires or dreams. We all have them, however big or small: they are what put our imaginations to work. So then what happens? We all have desires, but we all don't fulfill them. Why?

"Whether you think you can, or you think you can't, you're right."

— HENRY FORD

Brendan Burchard talks about the distinction between a successful mindset and one that doesn't lead to success. I'm fond of this line of thinking for two reasons: (1) a successful mindset starts from where? You got it — the Inside Out! And (2) the difference between a successful and unsuccessful mindset is very easy to understand but harder to embrace. The embracing part is, of course, your choice.

Burchard reminds us there is no trait for success. It isn't as if there is a gene for it. Rather, when it comes to success, it is more about how we manage our mind.

Perhaps you have a desire to be a successful entrepreneur. You want to own your own business. Then what happens? All the things you don't know start popping up…

- You don't know how to run a business.
- You don't have any capital.
- You don't know how, or have the money, to build a website to promote the business.

People who are not successful stop here, with all the things they don't have — the perceived "obstacles" that are in their way.

Successful people experience the same thing. They have a desire and then they have all the same thoughts about what's missing. So what's different? People with a successful mindset use the things they don't have as an action plan. They make a to-do list of what they need to learn how to do.

They know they can study successful entrepreneurs' stories, take business courses, and research online. They can learn about financing options, or how to build a website or a Facebook page to promote their new venture. They make a list, make a plan, create a timeline and go for it.

> The desire doesn't change. The mindset about how you approach something new and the action or inaction you take as a result is the difference.

What I recognized is that success is always about making conscious choices!

Carol S. Dweck devoted an entire book, *Mindset: The New Psychology of Success,* to identifying and illustrating the differences between the *fixed* mindset and the *growth* mindset. She said it began one day while she was working with one of her doctoral students as they were trying to understand why some students were so caught up in proving their ability while others could just let go and learn. They realized that people had two different views of ability. One view is that ability is *fixed.* You can't increase your ability; you can only prove that you have it. The other view is that ability is *changeable*; it can be developed through learning and practice, or *growth.* With this realization, Dweck understood why she had always been so concerned about mistakes and failures, and, as she said, she "recognized for the first time that she had a choice."

Success and living in alignment with our purpose passion and profit have to do with the ways we manage our mind and how we manage our days. It is always about making conscious choices.

CHOICE: Consistently Honing Our Intentions Concerning Excellence™

But how do we manage our choices? How do we recognize them? How do we get comfortable with owning them and taking responsibility for them? This is where the CHOICE model creates the framework for your ongoing maintenance. Using this framework allows you to develop and nurture the mindset you will need.

An action plan without the proper mindset will not prevail — and the proper mindset without an action plan for you to live by daily will not either. You will need both to keep you on track with your brand, being authentic, and living with purpose, passion and profit.

The CHOICE model identifies the six key elements that will guide your choices moving forward.

1. Consistently

The first key is being consistent. It's about keeping your antennae up and staying attuned, focused and practicing discipline. Consistency is a muscle that needs to be built to support you moving forward, as are the next two keys.

Where you are today is a culmination of all of your choices to date. What if your life's choices were held together by something? What if the choices you are making today would lead you to the life you truly desire tomorrow? They will lead you somewhere: will it be where you desire? If your choices are held together by your purpose, they will. Purpose is the glue to help you stay on track with the choices you are making consistently.

Think of purpose as having two levels. The first is *intrinsic / internal*. I call it our "way of being." As we discussed in Step One: Introspection, each of us has a unique and individualized way of being. The second level of purpose is *extrinsic*: it's the external expression of our unique way of being. I refer to this as our "way of doing." This is where purpose and choice intersect. Your choices will guide how you will (or won't) express your life's purpose.

> I want to invite you to really contemplate this vitally important thought: Your choices will guide how you will (or won't) express your life's purpose.

We cannot afford to make choices without thoughtful consideration as to how they affect our living in alignment — taking us ever closer to our desires, goals and purpose, or farther away.

Even seemingly small choices have enormous impact: from our self-talk, to what we eat, who we hang out with, our daily practices, how we interact with others, how we make time for self-care, how we reflect pride in our work, how we make our children feel loved, special and important consistently.

Managing ourselves to be on purpose demands a certain level of discipline. We need to stay informed, engaged, relevant and focused, and practice discipline if we are to build momentum.

Let me share an example or two of how this plays out in a very real application. I coach for a rapidly growing, large financial institution. And with growth comes new people, new values and new corporate cultural influences. On the one hand you have the "legacy" employees and management, and on the other you have the new hires. Oftentimes the legacy folks are the ones who implemented the procedures, policies and working processes currently in place. The legacy employees are attached to these procedures, maybe because they influenced their development or simply because they are familiar (and comfortable) with these ways of working.

Now enter the new hires, with their ideas, different experience sets, fresh suggestions and questioning current ways of doing things — all with good intent. Even so, they may experience pushback, resistance and even resentment from the legacy employees. This same dynamic occurs in many scenarios, not the least of which is mergers and acquisitions. It takes a smart company to not just let new hires "figure it out" but instead to actively call out the tension, acknowledge the cost of growth and get in front of the train to help people navigate together and get everyone operating as a newly expanded team.

Here are two notes I received from managers actively working to remain consistent in their daily activity. They want to be good leaders and role models and to provide help to their team. With that desire comes a commitment to consistent growth, re-examining themselves, being open to new learning and seeing how the team could work differently, better, in greater alignment with the team's goals.

Testimonial from Christian encouraging other managers:

"After completing our Assessments and learning more about our own styles, we had the chance to discuss the 'storming' we had been experiencing under my watch. I had the opportunity to learn more about one of my direct report's communication style, which is vastly different than mine. I also had the opportunity to learn how to adapt, and more importantly watched my direct report acknowledge their need to adapt to make the relationship work over the long haul.

"This level of consciousness is what I can personally attribute our uptick in productivity and teamwork to. If it were not for the few

weeks early on, we would not be prepared to grow our team or achieve everything on our plate this year."

Testimonial from Morgan:

"Anytime a conflict arises, our natural inclination is to think it is the other person who should have conducted themselves differently.

"Michele's one-on-one sessions allow you to air these opinions and frustrations before having your mind opened to the realization that you were just as much a part of the disagreement as the person you are experiencing communication troubles with is.

"All this time I thought that offering to help my colleagues upon hearing they were slammed with work was a positive thing. That was until I came across a colleague who took my offers as intruding on their territory. Working with Michele made me realize that I can still offer help but needed to word my offerings in a more humble way in order for it to be received as I intended.

"The next time I offered help I found that I was more successful in getting my coworker to let me in and be there for them in a time of need; without feeling like I was imposing on anything."

Both these managers are staying engaged. They have a growth mindset. They are willing to be self-reflective and willing to take action to be the best version of themselves for their teams. And their company invests in supporting their people to learn how to modify and manage the growth and change.

The Balance Between Staying Focused and Getting Stuck

There is a practical aspect to knowing your purpose, to following each of the steps in the brand building process and having certainty about the choices we make. There are many ways to express our purpose, to live with passion and to profit in the process. We live in a changing world. We must be ready to adjust — and it starts with a growth mindset. It's always ideal when we are able to anticipate by staying up to date and seeing what is relevant.

I have an interest in the human condition and contribution to others, and how that is affected (whether positively or negatively) by technology. I saw a recent article by Shelly Palmer that falls into the camp of staying relevant. Or, as I view it, how to think about your purpose and where you are able to best align it in pragmatic ways that allow you to profit. A few highlights from his article include:

- Research done by Oxford University estimates 47% of US jobs could be automated within the next 20 years — automated by machine learning algorithms running on purpose-built computer platforms, trained to perform tasks that currently require humans to perform.
- Palmer cites middle management as one of the arenas that may be automated. If your function is number crunching (moving data in and around spreadsheets), you are vulnerable. "Any job where your 'special and unique' knowledge of the industry is applied to divine a causal relationship between numbers in a matrix is going to be replaced first," he writes.
- Also soon to be replaced are salespeople for commodities (like ad sales and supplies, for example). This function can be accomplished by a request for proposal and

number crunching, all of which can be acquired online. *(My Note: If you are selling a service — one where your unique value proposition is important — that's another "sales" story altogether. In those circumstances, designing your brand to create demand is vital.)*

- A third area to re-think is report writers, journalists, authors and even announcers, Palmer says. Machines can be taught to read data, pattern match images or video, or analyze almost any kind of research materials and create very readable and / or announceable writing. Because text-to-speech systems are evolving so quickly, both play-by-play and color commentators can be replaced.

- Accountants and bookkeepers, beware: robo-accounting is in its infancy but is capable of handling accounts payable, receivable, inventory control and even auditing.

- Are you ready for this? Palmer even cites doctors as an occupation that could be replaced by technology. Diagnostic and surgery robots are already being used across cancer treatment, knee replacement and vision correction.

Part of nurturing and protecting your purpose is to consistently stay relevant and think ahead. This is how we grow as human beings. Maybe robots are actually going to ensure we accelerate our own growth by causing us to re-examine and hone our thinking. In any case, we need to remain consistent in our choices and anticipate, consciously plan and be willing to take action when it comes to learning things that are new.

This leads us into the next area of focus for maintenance and making aligned choices.

2. Honing

We have been talking about *consistently*, but in many aspects we've also tapped into the essence of *honing*. Honing invites you to reflect and re-invent, sharpen and fine-tune.

My journey to write the CHOICE model emerged by way of reflection and my determination to address people's desire to know how I was creating such sales success. My three-year, intensive, self-designed study program was about re-inventing myself to become a superb sales executive. Throughout that process I chose to consciously reflect and reexamine my beliefs, my habits, my dreams, my skills, my gaps, and actively design my brand by becoming a fuller, richer more purposeful version of myself.

The testimonial coaching stories I shared earlier reflect managers who are looking to sharpen their self-awareness and fine-tune their skills.

But this wouldn't have happened if their boss, Eric, hadn't been willing to do some honing of his own. He called me and we re-examined his strengths and gaps in his new Vice President role in that organization. He recognized through assessments, reflection and coaching he had tremendous strength in strategy and analyzing data. So, for example, he had crafted a sophisticated and innovative strategic plan for his department. However, he had gaps in his people skills, so instead of gaining buy-in by making the plan relevant for his team, he basically handed it out. It fell pretty flat.

He was perplexed. He knew it was a strong plan and thought it would cause enthusiasm amongst his team. Upon reflection, however, he recognized what he hadn't done to gain buy-in. He hadn't used what I call creating *Shared Perspective*:

looking at how you can impart something to positively impact someone from their point of view. Rather than create a roadmap everyone was excited by because they saw their role in it, he delivered a plan he expected them to execute upon.

To his great credit, he went back and re-engaged with his team. He made the plan meaningful and relevant for each team member. Today he has a team that has grown over 300% in 18 months and they are focused, driven and loyal.

His honing looked like this:

- While he and I worked through my *Communicate to Connect* program so he could elevate his communication skills, he brought me in to fill the people management gap to keep his team engaged on a daily basis. He saw the data and enacted strategy — he used his greatest strengths.
- He has masterminded one of the highest functioning teams I've ever worked with.
- He also continues to evolve his own leadership skills and has earned the respect of all who work for him.

I suspect throughout this book, with the various exercises and clicking through on the links to make use of key tools to help guide you, you've already engaged in honing as well. In fact, throughout this book as you've been reflecting, you've been honing.

- Maybe you've given thought to your purpose for the first time.
- Perhaps you are getting closer to or have identified your purpose.
- Maybe you identified some key markers about yourself in Introspection.

- Have you given new thought to how you see your value from your customer's point of view?
- If you are thinking about whether you simply communicate or if you are communicating to connect, you are honing.
- When you stopped to consider the most congruent way for you to create your brand buzz — that was honing.

Honing requires that you take the time (or make the time) to push "pause" on your reacting and doing and check in with yourself. Do you still have the same beliefs and thoughts about something? About yourself? Your purpose? Your career path? Are you energized or deflated by what you are choosing to engage in?

Honing tempts you into possibility, creativity and innovation. It taps into your imagination — my most favorite of human gifts, and I observe, the gift that is too often left unopened.

Another key area of importance when it comes to choice-driven maintenance is to *keep removing obstacles and barriers.* The easiest ones to remove are the ones outside of us: distancing ourselves from people that act as dream-stealers, for example, or leaving a job that is toxic (either to your internal spirit or by nature of the culture) or filling a gap by gaining necessary learning.

What are left are the obstacles that emanate from the Inside Out. This leads us to the third muscle we need to develop to navigate our choices purposefully.

3. Our

"Our" speaks to what we are actually in control of, which is ourselves. We simply cannot control or change another. At best, we can influence others; but ultimately it is they who will have to choose to make a change.

And yet, so many people spend their lives unknowingly or unconsciously hiding behind others. "If only he would... then I could..." Or, "If only they would... then I would be able to...." Or, "If she wouldn't... then I could...."

Where's the power in that mindset? It is all contingent upon others. That is what I mean by hiding behind someone else. If we went ahead and made choices for ourselves, independent of what others want, think, do, didn't do, will, won't... then we are in control. We can live in alignment with our own purpose.

When we don't, we live in a mindset of blame, victimhood, frustration, hurt and anger. These types of feelings are BIG clues we can recognize when we are honing, re-examining and re-thinking the dynamics of a situation, a relationship, a circumstance we find ourselves in. We can choose to not let these feelings go unchecked.

This is a topic of giant proportion. Much of my coaching is about guiding people to recognize that they have choices. They need to own their negative feelings so they can regain control over themselves. Then they can tap into their courage and move through the areas where they find themselves stuck or out of alignment with their purpose, their dreams or their stated goals.

But this is not a process we can do for anyone but ourselves. Every hour we spend trying to "fix" someone else or something else is an hour we take away from ourselves, and often this is used as an excuse, a manufactured distraction that prevents us from taking responsibility for ourselves.

> If you are not ready to receive, you won't see opportunity when it comes.

When we blame someone else, we are unconsciously choosing not to receive our own moment to grow. The easy way out, the fixed mindset, is one that surrenders to someone else's wants, desires, dictates. The courageous step is to be ready to change, to grow, to step up and meet what is put before you.

One way to recognize this opportunity is to ask yourself right now, who are you currently blaming... for anything? Then you get to go into a place of honing and ask yourself (or someone else, if you don't know), how can you move from being stuck to taking your next step forward?

Taking responsibility, taking ownership, is about regaining control of ourselves. While "hour" and "our" may sound alike, they are entirely different in the context of our relationship to time and to being in alignment with our purpose, passion and profit. Only the hour we spend looking for our part in something is time well spent.

Time is your most precious gift: don't squander it with poor choices! You can go broke and regain riches. You can suffer the loss of someone and find new love. But you can never regain time. It is finite! Choose to make yours count by consistently making choices that keep you in (or redirect you back into) alignment.

4. Intentions

Without a solid framework around you and a strong foundation beneath you it won't matter what you intend to do, have or be. Your intentions will show up only as wishes. The CHOICE framework will act as your guide, and the first three keys to making good choices — Consistently, Honing and Our — are the muscles that will support you.

With these pieces in place, it's time for clarity of your *intentions*. Clarity creates possibility. What is your vision for yourself? Short term? Long term?

However, you can intend all day long to win the lottery, but if you don't make money to buy a ticket, or if you don't plan when you need to purchase before the drawing takes place and if you don't take the action of going to buy the ticket, you're not going to win the lottery.

The same is true with intention. By consciously embracing consistency, you build momentum. You have the discipline it takes to break through barriers, to overcome challenges or, once in place, to sustain successes achieved. Through honing you continue to evolve: to be reflective, to be self-aware, to grow and stretch, to develop new talents and improve existing skills. And by learning to look inside and take responsibility in all situations you gain the control to stay focused, on purpose and minimize distractions.

With these muscles developed you have the foundation that can support your intentions, which are the visions that color your dreams, inspire your aspirations and drive your goals. Said another way, with a strong foundation, your intentions can be supported by your choices, your vision and your strategy.

Strategy is what puts your intention into action! Your choices can reflect your intentions and steer them into becoming reality.

The clearer you are, the more focused you will be able to be. And when you focus you will find you have fewer (although well-selected) choices to manage.

Fulfillment of Your Purpose Happens One CHOICE at a Time

I have both personally experienced and professionally observed that getting clarity — that is, knowing with absolute certainty what you want — is often as hard or harder than achieving the goal you are clear about. This is another reason why Step One: Introspection, is so powerful. It begins to activate that clarity.

The power of your intention unleashes your imagination. When you have clarity around your purpose, the innate power and creativity of your imagination can align and drive you into possibilities and outcomes you will find astounding! With imagination, I have achieved things I never thought possible. And I know that the momentum continues to build and the best is yet to come!

I also know that if our intentions are not crystal clear we can intend one thing and manifest another. I learned this lesson firsthand over 25 years ago when I was attending a workshop called Competitive Winning. It was a week of self-reflection and honing in action, designed to help you learn how you go about winning.

For one exercise the entire group was split into two teams. Each team was to complete a crossword puzzle together. The exercise was to see which team could come together best to finish the task quickest. I wanted to not only beat the other team but also to break the record, so I asked what the fastest completion time was to date. The workshop instructors said 12 minutes and 39 seconds. I then announced and wrote down that our team would complete the puzzle in 12:38.

As soon as we heard the word, "Start!" part of our team began discussing who would write the letters in, while others on the team jumped in and starting guessing the words. There wasn't much of a strategy: those who were most vocal emerged quickly, while others in the team just looked on. The process seemed fairly haphazard.

"Done!" the other team shouted. Done? We weren't even halfway finished! We struggled through, frustrations rising, and then finally we were done. Not only hadn't we beaten the other team, but we actually took 42 minutes, 38 seconds to complete the puzzle — the longest time on record!

When we had finished, one of the instructors asked me to look at the clock. The time on the clock astonished me, and I wanted to crawl in a hole. It was 12:38 p.m. — exactly what I had written down. What I had *intended* was to complete the puzzle in 12 minutes and 38 seconds, but what transpired was not at all what I had intended. And the instructor said she knew the minute she saw how I wrote the time down what was going to occur.

This exercise illustrates how incredibly powerful each of us is. We must not only be clear as to what we want (in this case to beat the team and the overall record) but we must declare what we intend with great clarity as well.

I've never forgotten this lesson. I'm very mindful of being clear on what I intend and declaring it with thoughtfulness. A simple example of this occurs when people declare that they intend to lose weight. If they just say, "I intend to lose 10 pounds," they could do so by becoming ill. I doubt getting sick was what they intended, but that may be what transpires. Instead, people need to be specific about the amount they wish to lose and in what fashion: "I intend to lose 10 pounds over the next three months in a healthy manner," for example.

Start With Intention — the "How" Will Follow

The process of intention is to declare it and then get out of the way. Identify "what" you intend initially and don't censor yourself with the "how." Many people with an imagination along with a growth mindset didn't know how they were going to succeed: they just had a desire and an intention. A few examples: the Wright Brothers, Marie Curie, Albert Einstein, Mahatma Gandhi, Louis Braille, Rosa Parks, Leonardo da Vinci, Sally Ride, Benjamin Franklin, Steve Jobs, Oprah Winfrey, Ellen DeGeneres, Elon Musk… and the list goes on.

Here is a pragmatic illustration of how this plays out on a daily basis, when a client, Kiley, needed to focus on the "what" so she wouldn't get derailed and fall off the "how" cliff.

I hold "Open Office Hours" for my corporate clients; this allows individuals in the organization to call in for confidential coaching at prescribed times. These sessions begin with them sending me a "heads up" note the day before regarding the items they want to cover in our call. This gets them focused and gives me time to prepare where needed.

Background:

The note I received from Kiley said she had two issues she wanted to discuss: "(1) I'm being pulled in from other departments to help with projects and I am overwhelmed; I cannot get my work done. (2) My own team is pulling me in on projects and I can't get my work done there either. These projects are outside my core area of responsibility, if you will."

My note back to her read: "It sounds like you want to have a conversation around boundaries." She agreed.

What I know:

I've already discussed and provided links to the tools I use when I'm coaching that allow me to assess someone's styles of behavior and their motivators. When I understand these, I know how to best accommodate them and connect with them from their point of view.

This client is a people person (she likes to engage) and a people pleaser (she doesn't want to disappoint). I know going in that she doesn't want to say no. She isn't comfortable saying no and she doesn't know how to do so. This is why she is stuck and reaching out for guidance.

Boundaries versus re-framing:

I started by asking her, "Do you want to say no to the demand that is being created for your involvement?" Her answer was that she liked being involved and working on these projects; she just couldn't get her own work done.

I suggested that it was possible she didn't need to say no, and we could explore some other ways to look at this. "Do you have anybody else that reports to you that you could get some help from?" She replied that there was no one available and no "head count allotted" (no budget assigned for hiring someone).

I then asked her how she felt about moving away from being an individual contributor and maybe being *quasi* hands-on and *quasi* oversight. She said, "I'd be open to that, but we don't have any open head count."

Intentions require we focus on the "what," not the "how," initially. I told her, "Okay, I get why you can't. Let's just stay with the idea of what's desirable. Are you willing to do that?" When she agreed, I asked her to talk to me for a moment about her internal clients. "Who is it that's creating the demand for you? Where are you being pulled in to?" She answered that it was XYZ department, ABC department and LMNOP department that all were looking for different help.

Because I coach across the entire corporation, I know things that individuals within the company may not have exposure to. So I was able to say to her (without breaking any confidences), "Here's what I know. XYZ department happens to be the fastest growing department in your entire organization. They have enormous resources being put behind them. So what if you were to go to them and say, 'Hey XYZ department, I appreciate that you're getting so much value out of what I've been providing to you. It took a little while for us to get going but now we're humming along here, and I like that you want me to contribute. Here's the thing: I'm running out of bandwidth. I was wondering, how important is my being involved to you? What are the costs if we don't move fast or forward with what we've got going on? What's the opportunity if we do? How significant is what we're working on in terms of what you need to get where you want to go?'"

Then I suggested that she let them answer. They might say, "You know what, actually we can wait. Maybe next year you'll get head count. We're good." If so, it's now off her plate. She wouldn't have to say no: they just handled it for her.

On the other hand, they might say, "Yes, actually it's really important. We really want this. We're realizing how important it really is." Then she could tee up this opportunity: "Listen, I don't have the resources. Can you guys think about putting in for a new head count? Can you get somebody on board that I can mold, model, teach and show how to do it? I can manage them and continue to oversee it: I can support you at that level. I won't go away. I'll make sure it's done right, but can you get the head count?"

I reminded her, "If they say yes, you've already said that you'll support it. You're good to go. You feel better, and they're happy. If they say no, again, it's off your plate. Sometimes what we think needs to be a boundary is just because we don't know what else to do. In truth, a boundary, which has a dotted line to a 'no' behind it, could instead be a reframe of possibility, which has a dotted line to a 'yes' behind it. If you're struggling trying to say no, let's figure out if there is another way that you could look at it so you can say yes."

Boundaries vs. Re-framing

"No"   "Yes"

If you have an intention, explore the possibilities of "how." There's always a way! It may not be a straight line. It may involve trial and failure. But that is part of the process of moving closer in alignment with our purpose.

If everyone gave up on their intentions because they didn't know how, the world would be operating with a fixed mindset and humanity might never have seen man take flight, or a two-time female Nobel prize winner in two sciences leading us to today's x-ray machines. We might never have identified the law of gravity, developed the Braille language, seen the first woman in space, have electricity, or individual computers on our desks and smartphones in our hands.

Whether our intentions are on a grand scale doesn't matter: what does matter is that we gain clarity on what our intentions are, use a growth mindset to see possibility and allow that to take us ever closer toward our purpose, passion and profit.

One of the offers we make available to our workshop participants is the Intentions Exercise, designed so people can see the power of their intentions. It is very simply a sheet that asks people to get clear on what they intend to do, have or be in the next 30 days. They write it down and give it to us to return to them in 30 days.

Many times people are concerned that if they hand over their list they won't know what they wrote down. But the point of the exercise is this: when you truly intend something and you thoughtfully declare it, things will start to align and take you in that direction. Your only job is to be very clear about what you sincerely intend and then to let it occur — meaning, don't get in the way either because you are distracted or you are trying to direct it and then you miss the miracles that are being put before you to help you manifest your intention.

(If you would like to do this exercise yourself, just go to **Skilset.com/intentions** and you can fill out your intentions and send it to us. We will be the custodians and return it to you in 30 days. Try it and you'll see how it works!)

Once you've built your muscles and gained perspective and strength in the quality of your choices, you realize that aligning with your purpose usually involves an awareness of how you are impacting others.

Let me use the example of this book. My company has had two divisions, one of which focuses on coaching and training. And while I've been consciously and positively affecting people through workshops and coaching for over two decades, writing a book was not something I ever felt was the best use of my time and focus when it came to my company's overall goals.

One day I decided to apply what I was teaching and I went back onto my own journey to clarify my purpose, which is to *guide companies and their individuals to reach unimaginable outcomes by aligning their purpose, passion and profit.* Based on this realization, I knew that the work that really filled my soul was what I was doing in the coaching and training division of my business and I committed to putting more of my focus there. I also became clear that I wanted to vastly expand the reach of my impact on others. With that clarity came the intention to get this book written.

When the clarity of your intention becomes your vision, then you know that you are fully owning your purpose and ready to make a meaningful difference in the world. That is what Concerning is all about.

5. Concerning

I'm reminded of a 50/50 bar when I think about *concerning*. A 50/50 bar is an ice cream bar that is half vanilla ice cream at the center with another half on the outside that is orange popsicle... thus the name 50/50.

I see this as a metaphor for Concerning in the CHOICE model. When we first delve into the discovery of our purpose, we are by definition going on an internal discovery. This, reminds me of the vanilla ice cream at the center of the 50/50 bar. At first we are trying to reach our center, to figure out what we are meant for, what we are motivated by, how we go about things — looking for clues and cues to help us recognize what that purpose is.

The orange popsicle on the outside is the second half of the discovery, which is identifying why we have this purpose and how we can affect others with it. The second half shows up when we are ready and capable of being of real value to others.

You could liken it to the announcement you hear aboard every flight: "In case of emergency, please put your oxygen mask on first and then assist your child." If you aren't safe, you won't be able to help your child. If you don't recognize your purpose, you won't be able to be of greatest value to others.

Interestingly, this metaphor is actually quite literal. When you recognize and fully own your purpose it provides an enormous sense of safety. You know with certainty you are not only doing the right things but you are supported in ways that seem beyond your own efforts. Opportunities show up, people show up, you rise to new heights. While on the surface you may need to muster some courage to believe in yourself and be as great as you are intended to be, underlying this is a knowing, an inner peacefulness, a calm, a feeling that you have a safety net woven of the same miracle that you yourself are!

This doesn't mean you won't have challenges or obstacles — quite the contrary. They too are part of that fabric of miracles put there precisely for you to overcome and to allow you to grow into your next best version of yourself.

Concerning is a concept that is pragmatically demonstrated by being a congruent individual: someone who is solid, internally filled up with the riches of knowing your purpose and aligning it with your passions and talents, who has the capacity and the wisdom to be of value to others.

This shows up when you are doing what you are meant to do. When I am holding a workshop, coaching a receptive client who is committed to their growth, or when I am writing what touches my heart and I know can touch others' hearts as well, I am in the flow, in the zone. In this state I could literally "work," standing in heels, without eating, for 24 to 48 or more hours with energy and focus. There are periods when I'm working where it feels as if it's only been a moment or two when in fact it has been hours. I feel like I am doing the work but it's almost as if it's just passing through me — it feels absolutely effortless and at the same time wholly energizing.

No one can skip the process of making Consistently Honed Intentions and just leap ahead to being Concerned for others in a valuable and sustainable way. We likely feel that there are people in our lives for whom we wish to demonstrate concern for their well-being. If so, then it is necessary for us to first make a commitment to ourselves, to learn the process of making good and inspired choices. We must be that which we wish to offer to another. We must model. Be authentic. Be whole. We cannot guide or support others until we first put on our own oxygen mask.

> Potential is a CHOICE waiting to happen.

Ultimately, the very reason we learn and practice the process of making aligned choices is for the purpose of giving it away, contributing to others, making a difference with our lives. While there certainly is joy in discovery, there is an indescribable joy in sharing what we have learned, being a model, being a leader who has the capacity to be concerned for others. This is when we get to recognize we are fulfilling our full potential.

I invite you to get started, or continue moving forward, depending on where you are in your journey.

6. Excellence

To me, living in *excellence* means being and doing our own personal best. It is the final piece in the way we can think about the choices we are making to keep us in alignment with our purpose and keep our brand authentic and continuously in demand.

Excellence is NOT perfection. Perfection is the antithesis of excellence, as it often causes paralysis. The intimidation is so great that one cannot get started for fear of being less than their expectation.

Excellence requires that fear be worked through and not avoided. Excellence demands that we are strong, exercising courage even in the face of fear, resilient, unbending in our efforts to be our best.

Excellence requires we take control and think creatively and strategically toward breakthrough.

Excellence inherently acts as a mirror to others and either serves to inspire or intimidate. We must be willing to respond to inspiration by continuously living as our best self, a role model, and intimidation by handling other's fear and anger with compassion if they react that way to our living as our best selves.

It is possible to be in a process of excellence in some areas of our lives and not in others. Some of these areas are: communication skills, compassion for others, controlling our emotions, making conscious choices, ability to focus, work performance, time management, financial security, physical health, creative expression, relationships (i.e., parent/child, spouse, co-workers, authority figures) — you get the idea.

Part of your successful CHOICE process will be to identify which areas you need to focus on at any given time. You will be guided internally by being introspective — becoming quiet and being reflective.

The CHOICE process continues throughout our lives. As we move through one cycle of choices we arrive at a new place. Or we may literally arrive at the same physical place but with a new mind, a new set of experiences, a new understanding. This is how we continue to grow and get closer to being the best version of ourselves. For instance, I am not the same person I was before the death of my mother or the events leading up to her passing. I may engage in the same activities — work, friends, writing — but I see them differently, from a new perspective. It influences my work, how I view friends and what I write about.

While it's not possible to do justice to the CHOICE model and its impact in one chapter of this book, the overall elements and how they work have been laid out so you can use them to guide you moving forward and support you in daily maintenance on your journey.

And for those who wanted me to write the CHOICE book first, please know there's more to come. This is the subject of my next book, *The Power of CHOICE from the Inside Out.* In the meantime we also offer CHOICE webinars, workshops and retreats to guide you and provide you with hands-on support.

Excellence calls on us to live our lives as an art, a creative process, wherein CHOICE acts as our paintbrush.

About Michele Lando

President & Co-founder, Skilset Communications, Inc.

By using her unique approach, Michele guides companies and their individuals to reach unimaginable outcomes by aligning their Purpose, Passion and Profit.

It was in 1994 that Michele Lando co-founded Skilset Communications with the purpose of guiding companies such as Akamai Technologies, American Express, Bank of America, Bosley Medical, Cisco Systems, Cedars-Sinai Hospital, Metropolitan Water District, Prudential Retirement, US Trust, Visa, and Wells Fargo, to name a few, to reach their full potential.

As a coach, Michele looks for ways to enhance the perception of her clients in their marketplace. She helps leadership align internal philosophies, behaviors and messages to create strength in the brand via congruency. As a result, she positively influences corporate cultures as well.

Michele believes that treating clients as business *partners* increases accountability and joy in the working relationship and is essential to delivering beyond expectations.

Her methodology is unique. Michele looks at everyone, and each objective they have, from the Inside Out. She walks her talk. She brings science, tools and wisdom to each client.

Prior to launching Skilset Communications Inc., Michele was a highly successful sales strategist (a top 2% female earner nationally by age 28). She then developed and delivered her first global marketing training program to thousands of worldwide sales associates of a Fortune 500 firm, achieving unprecedented results.

Since that time Michele has authored and delivered numerous programs, including her international *IndiBrand™* training program, the *CHOICE™* series, *Communicate to Connect* and *DISCovering the Value of Your Team*, along with countless leadership, sales and communications programs. Most recently, she became a Bestselling Author.

All of her coaching and training work is customized and takes various forms to ensure a maximized return on investment for each of her clients. As a popular speaker herself, she is often asked to provide her clients speaker coaching.

Additionally, with the rising popularity of TED talks, Michele was asked to be a speaker coach for TEDx two years running, activating some exceptional and popular talent.

Michele has held seats on a variety of boards. She grew up in Los Angeles and her formal education was at UCLA (go Bruins!). She continues to reside in Los Angeles today with her husband and best friend of 30 years. They enjoy European travel — favoring Portugal!

Hire Michele To Speak At Your Event!

Book Michele Lando as your keynote speaker and you're guaranteed to make your event highly engaging and empowering!

For over two decades, Michele Lando has been educating, inspiring and guiding professional services entrepreneurs, corporate executives, sales professionals, consultants and coaches to build and grow their acumen and their businesses.

Her origin story includes...

- her sales job failure turned into career recovery, resulting in becoming a Top 2% earner by age 28
- a temporary job that lasted 14 years and included a seat on the board
- launching her own entrepreneurial venture at 35
- the "you have 6 months to live" conversation that changed her life forever
- a devastating personal loss, leading to innovating tools and programs to engage, ignite and transform those hungry to grow and sustain businesses — no matter the obstacles — and, in fact, because of them

After successfully building her own businesses and learning how to use them as living laboratories for her own success, Michele Lando can share relevant, actionable strategies that anyone can use, whether highly seasoned professionals or starting a venture from scratch, to unlock the keys to their greatest success.

Her unique style inspires and empowers audiences while giving them the practical tools and strategies they need to create demand for themselves, their companies and their teams.

For more information, visit **Skilset.com/speakingforsuccess** or call +1 (626) 792-0032.

About Skilset Programs and Workshops

Skilset recognizes that an organization's brand is made up of parts but is seen as a whole. That's why our coaching programs are designed to help everyone across your organization. We guide individuals, departments and corporate leaders to help them make conscious, well-designed choices that achieve their most important business goals.

Logistics of Customized Coaching Program Design

Each of our coaching programs is customized to the needs of the individual and the organization. They are designed to meet the needs of the desired goals and in the timeframes needed. They may run three, six, twelve months in duration. Sessions may be designed for 2 hours or 1 hour. Some clients prefer a retainer relationship to meet a team or division goal and/or often times we have clients who want access to on-going support on an as-needed basis.

Leadership Coaching

We cultivate leaders who can effectively navigate change, overcome obstacles, and create followership among stakeholders. By aligning the power of a leader's personal brand with a company's mission, values, and strategies, our coaching delivers exponential business impact. Very simply, what we do works!

"You add value in ways you don't even realize. Thank you for your contribution to me and the organization as we've grown so rapidly these past two years."

Bill Page, President Merisel Open Computing Alliance

ExecuBrand™

We help C-level executives, senior executives and vice presidents in *Fortune* 50 corporations and mid-sized companies achieve their most important objectives. We work together to clarify their purpose, their positioning, and their key messaging to build their brand awareness, visibility, and cachet in their organization, their industry, and in the marketplace. We collaborate on strategic, pragmatic application and execution to create powerful, ongoing connection with each of their stakeholders — be it boards, managers, clients, employees, other industry leaders, country leaders, or international media.

Communications Coaching for Departments and Divisions

Departments and divisions become their own sub-brands within an organization, sparking a positive, negative or neutral reputation. Skilset works with division leaders, their teams, and their individual employees, to create awareness, develop strategy, and implement tools that enhance the way they work. In doing so, they elevate their own reputation and gain positive mindshare in the organization, a stronger voice at the table, more robust budgets being allocated to meet their goals, and overall support throughout the company. The result for the organization as a whole is greater performance and enhanced outcomes.

"...I have thought about how much I have learned from you and how much value you have brought me over the years. You provided much thoughtful advice and challenged me to think about some things I would never have considered."

David S. Hauptman, Senior Vice President
MullinTBG, A Prudential Financial company

Organizational/Cultural Coaching

Working with thousands of individuals over 20 years, we have witnessed, experienced, and concluded people want to be stimulated, to learn, to grow, to contribute fully. To become ambassadors of an organization, employees, management, executives, and the C-suite need to feel an emotional connection to their corporate brand. We help you build those connections. From there, a culture is created, an engaging brand is developed across all stakeholder interactions, and a momentum for sustained success is in play.

Executive Sales Coaching

Sales success is a matter of consistent honing and refinement of skills. Through our coaching, sales executives evolve their mindset, adopt the skills, and instill the behaviors that help their clients, prospects, and centers of influence feel connected to and fully aligned with them as a partner. Your sales executives come away with new perspectives, refined processes, redefined beliefs, and immediate actionability. As a result they learn how to create sustainable, elevated sales relationships and measurable results.

"In six sessions, Michele helped me to close an \$11M deal. One might think that was the highlight of my experience with her. In reality, she did more! She helped me 'get my head on right.' I fully recommend anyone who has the chance to be coached by Michele take full advantage of the opportunity!"

J. S., SVP Private Client Advisor U.S. Trust

To learn more about Michele's IndiBrand and CHOICE workshops, please go to www.skilset.com

References

Dweck, Carol S., Ph.D., *Mindset: The New Psychology of Success* (New York: Random House, 2006).

Koenigs, Mike. *Publish and Profit: A 5-Step System for Attracting Paying Coaching and Consulting Clients, Traffic and Leads, Product Sales and Speaking Engagements* (San Diego: MikeKoenigs.com Inc., 2012).

Palmer, Shelly (February 26, 2017). The 5 jobs robots will take first [online]. LinkedIn article. Retrieved April 7, 2017 from https://www.linkedin.com/pulse/5-jobs-robots-take-first-shelly-palmer

Periu, Omar, *Network Your Way to the Top* (Boca Raton, FL: Omar Periu International, Inc., 2013). Versions of the 7 top networking questions can be found on p. 12.

Pink, Daniel H., *To Sell is Human: The Surprising Truth About Moving Others* (New York: Riverhead Books, 2012).

Rainie, Lee and Perrin, Andrew (October 19, 2015). Slightly fewer Americans are reading print books, new survey finds [online]. Pew Research Center. Retrieved April 8, 2017 from http://www.pewresearch.org/fact-tank/2015/10/19/slightly-fewer-americans-are-reading-print-books-new-survey-finds/.

Tracy, Reid (2017). Finding something to write about. *Present moments* newsletter [online]. Sent via email March 12, 2017 from hayhouse@email-hayhouse.com.